Reviving Regulatory Reform

Reviving Regulatory Reform

A Global Perspective

Robert W. Hahn

AEI-Brookings Joint Center for Regulatory Studies

WASHINGTON, D.C.
2000

To order call toll free 1-800-462-6420 or 1-717-794-3800. For all other inquiries please contact the AEI Press, 1150 Seventeenth Street, N.W., Washington, D.C. 20036 or call 1-800-862-5801.

Library of Congress Cataloging-in-Publication Data

Hahn, Robert W.

      Reviving regulatory reform: a global perspective / Robert W. Hahn
         p. cm.
Includes bibliographical references and index.
      ISBN 0-8447-4121-3 (alk. paper) – ISBN 0-8447-4122-1
      (pbk.: alk. paper)
      1. Privatization. 2. Deregulation. I. Title
      HD3850 .H24 2000
      338.9–dc21   00-045107

ISBN 0-8447-4121-3 (alk. paper)
ISBN 978-0-8447-4122-2 (pbk.: alk. paper)

1 3 5 7 9 10 8 6 4 2

The AEI Press
Publisher for the American Enterprise Institute
1150 17th Street, N.W.
Washington, D.C. 20036

For Juliette Hahn

Contents

Acknowledgments   xi

1 Reviving Regulatory Reform   1

2 Regulation and Its Reform around the World   6

   The Definition of, Rationale for, and Problems with Regulation 7
   The Benefits and Costs of Regulation 9
   Trends in Economic Regulation and Privatization 13
   Trends in Social Regulation 21
   Recent Attempts at Reforming the Regulatory Process 22
   Conclusions 29

3 Regulatory Reform: Assessing the U.S. Government's Numbers   32

   How Complete Are the Government's Numbers? 34
   What Do the U.S. Government's Numbers Tell Us? 38
   Statutory Restrictions on Regulations and Economic Efficiency 54
   The Influence of Regulatory Impact Analyses on the Regulatory
       Process 57
   Conclusions and Policy Recommendations 63

4 The Internationalization of Regulatory Reform   65

   Important Factors Affecting the Structure of Regulatory Reform 65

Whither Regulatory Reform? 69
International Aspects of Regulatory Reform 74
Conclusion 77

Notes   79

References   101

Index   113

About the Author   119

Figures
2-1   Pollution Abatement and Control Expeditures as a Percentage of GDP 13
2-2   Privatization in OECD Countries 14
2-3   Deregulation of Entry Restrictions in OECD Countries 15
2-4   Deregulation of Price Restrictions in OECD Countries 16
2-5   Ownership of Service Industries in Developing Countries 17
2-6   Regulation of Service Industries in Developing Countries 18
2-7   Ownership of Product Industries in Developing Counties 19
2-8   Regulation of Product Industries in Developing Countries 20
3-1   Net Benefits of Final Major Regulations as a Function of Time, 1981–1997 45
3-2   Aggregate Net Benefits of Final Regulations as a Function of the Discount Rate 47
3-3   Cost-Effectiveness of Selected Final Environmental, Health, and Safety Regulations 48
3-4   Cost-Effectiveness of Selected Environmental, Health, and Safety Regulations 51

Tables
2-1   Costs of Regulation and Projected Benefits of Deregulation as a Percentage of GDP 12
2-2   Overview of Regulatory Reform Efforts around the World 23
2-3   Review of Existing Regulatory Activities and Procedures 24
2-4   Recent U.S. Initiatives to Review New Regulatory Activity 26
2-5   Recent U.S. Initiatives to Review Existing Regulation 27
2-6   Recent U.S. Legislation with Greater Emphasis on Balancing Benefits and Costs 28
2-7   Overview of Regulatory Reform Efforts in Selected States 30
3-1   Regulatory Scorecard, 1981 to Mid-1996 36

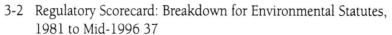
3-2 Regulatory Scorecard: Breakdown for Environmental Statutes, 1981 to Mid-1996 37

3-3 Key Parameters of the Model 40

3-4 Net Benefits of Regulations, 1981 to Mid-1996 42

3-5 Net Benefits of Regulations: Breakdown for Environmental Statutes, 1981 to Mid-1996 43

3-6 Sensitivity Analysis of the Net Benefits of Final Rules 46

3-7 Regression Results 49

3-8 Statutory Treatment of Balancing 56

3-9 Rules Passing a Benefit-Cost Test 58

3-10 Number of Rules Passing a Benefit-Cost Test 59

3-11 Federal Regulatory Agencies' Efforts to Catalog Benefit and Cost Information 62

Acknowledgments

This book is part of a continuing effort aimed at understanding and improving regulation. Part of this effort culminated in the launching of the AEI-Brookings Joint Center for Regulatory Studies, which I have the privilege of directing. My hope is that this book and the efforts of the Joint Center will help illuminate an arcane area of inquiry that frequently has more impact on people than they realize.

Many colleagues have contributed to the ideas in this book. I would like to thank Jason Burnett, Irene Chan, Chris DeMuth, Art Fraas, Harold Furchtgott-Roth, Luis Guach, Randall Kroszner, John Morrall, Robert Litan, Randall Lutter, Al McGartland, Petrea Moyle, Roger Noll, Jonathan Siskin, Clifford Winston, and Fumie Yokata for their constructive feedback and insights. I would also like to thank Ed Dale and Leigh Tripoli for excellent editorial support and Mark Steinmeyer for continued encouragement. The final product represents my views and not necessarily the views of anyone else.

Reviving Regulatory Reform

1

Reviving Regulatory Reform

Markets are becoming increasingly popular around the world. Perhaps the most notable transitions to a market-oriented economy are taking place in China, the former Soviet Union, and the eastern bloc countries, nations that at one time embraced communism. But the reach of markets is also growing in a variety of other nations, such as Mexico, Chile, and Uganda. Scholars and policymakers no longer seriously debate the ability of market economies to outperform centrally planned economies. The renewed interest in markets has given rise to a set of economic policies that recast the role of the state. For example, interest in privatizing state-owned enterprises has been increasing worldwide.

Something similar is happening in the move to reform government regulation, although policy analysts generally agree that the state will continue to play an important role in regulating specific economic activities. Around the world, analysts are debating issues related to the form and extent of regulation. Those issues differ across countries, however. For example, in developed countries the question is often how best to reform an existing regulatory structure; in contrast, in developing countries the question is often how to design a regulatory structure almost from scratch. Both scholars and practitioners are devising innovative solutions to the problem of regulatory design.

Policymakers are engaged in a continuing, thorough reexamination of how national and state governments regulate areas ranging from telecommunications to the environment. So extensive is the questioning of the familiar, and so daring some of the proposed and actual changes, that the movement deserves the term *revolution,* just as the move toward markets and privatization in national economies deserves that term.

A deeper understanding of the economic and social impacts of regulation is fueling the regulatory revolution. People are becoming more aware that regulations impose costs on individuals, even if those costs are hidden from view, as is the case with most regulation. Changes in the economic benefits and costs of regulation that technology has induced are also driving the revolution. For example, it is now economically feasible to have "pay TV" and to have telephone conversations that use the spectrum or the Internet instead of a central exchange. Those technological innovations increase the cost of maintaining the existing regulatory structure and thus create pressure for change.[1] Finally, improvements in monitoring outputs and behavior are propelling the revolution. Smart cards placed in vehicles allow governments to charge travelers for driving during peak hours; we can now measure pollution in real time for many industrial processes; and electric utilities can send rapidly changing price signals to businesses at low cost and perhaps can soon do so for households.

We need to examine the revolution in regulation not only in terms of its impact on national economies, but also in terms of its potential international effects. For example, stringent regulation of the environment in one country may induce firms to relocate to other countries. In addition, product specifications introduced under the guise of protecting consumers may give domestic producers a competitive advantage.[2] Thus, regulation can dramatically influence the pattern of international trade and investment. For example, the World Trade Organization ruled that a U.S. regulation for cleaner gasoline constituted a trade barrier that should be removed.[3] At the international level, nations are seriously discussing an environmental treaty to limit greenhouse gases.

The international ramifications of domestic regulation are likely to increase in importance as markets become more global. The growth in the size of markets is an inevitable result of the decreasing costs of transportation and communication. Capital can be now be moved halfway around the world with one keystroke.[4] Just as nations have attempted to coordinate their activities in an effort to reduce direct trade barriers such as tariffs, they may also need to coordinate some regulatory activities that distort patterns of trade and investment.

The United States is in the vanguard of the regulatory revolution. Both Democrats and Republicans are placing increasing emphasis on the need for reform. And while the individuals and parties have different notions of how to implement reform, the degree of consensus is surprising. For example, politicians and the general public are becoming increasingly aware of the paperwork burden that both federal and state regulations impose. They are also growing more sensitive to the large number of counterproductive regulations.[5] Several years ago, former senator and Democratic presidential candidate George McGovern opened an inn in Connecticut to fulfill a lifelong dream. The inn eventually went bankrupt. McGovern told his tale of woe in a *Wall Street Journal* op-ed, where he blamed part of the failure of the inn on the needless red tape and excessive costs that regulations impose.[6]

But the concerns about regulation and the appropriate form of regulation extend beyond the United States.[7] An array of developed and developing countries are now implementing and beginning to evaluate several regulatory reforms. For example, the government of Mexico has launched an ambitious program aimed at simplifying regulation so that it is easier for small and medium-sized enterprises to do business. That is not an isolated example. Britain is undertaking an extensive review of existing regulations, and several states in Australia are using economic analysis to develop a more effective and efficient regulatory process.

Scholars and journalists continue to assemble and analyze examples of regulatory successes and failures. For example, a recent review of government regulatory analyses of major federal regulations found that very few consider alternatives or quantify the net benefits of the regulation.[8] An earlier examination of several regulatory impact analyses suggested that in some cases the analyses led to improvements in the actual regulation.[9] An examination of proposed changes in noise standards for aircraft found that they would be unlikely to increase economic welfare by much.[10] Those studies appeared after Philip Howard's *Death of Common Sense,* a 1995 bestseller that chronicled regulation gone awry.[11]

The scholarly literature is consistent with many of the stories that the press has recounted, although the findings tend to be more balanced. Researchers have shown that price and entry regulation of specific industries—known as *economic regulation*—has tremendous costs. For example, Hahn and Hird estimated the total annual cost of that type of regulation at $55 billion.[12] A subsequent estimate by Winston that uses a different baseline places the number at $24 billion annually.[13]

Environmental, health, and safety regulation—called *social regulation*—has both benefits and costs.[14] While some environmental, health, and safety rules have clearly been beneficial, such as the phasedown of lead in gasoline, growing evidence shows that many recent laws and regulations would not pass a benefit-cost test. For example, economists estimated that the 1990 Clean Air Act Amendments would impose a net cost on the economy of about $15 billion annually when fully implemented.[15] My analysis of federal regulations between 1981 and mid-1996 reveals that only about 43 percent of 106 final regulations examined would pass a neutral economist's benefit-cost test.[16]

It is important to be clear about the nature of the regulatory revolution.

It is *not* solely about deregulation, although that is an important component. The revolution is about selecting both the right regulatory tool and the right regulatory goal.[17] Even when considerations of economic efficiency make deregulation of an industry the preferred policy, the state has an important role to play in limiting anticompetitive practices through instruments such as antitrust.

In many cases, the right tool will be one that affords maximum flexibility in reaching the goal, so that one can tap into the ingenuity of the marketplace. For example, instead of specifying the height of railings for factories producing bricks, the Occupational Safety and Health Administration could inform those factories of the kinds of business practices and equipment that appear to improve workplace safety. Then, firms could tailor that information to their particular needs. Similarly, governments could follow the U.S. example of using a market-based approach, sometimes called emissions trading, to reduce sulfur dioxide emissions that cause acid rain. Such flexible approaches have the potential to save billions of dollars annually while achieving more ambitious regulatory goals.

From an economist's perspective, the selection of the right goal should be based on the benefits and costs of a policy, although that may not be the sole criterion.[18] A review of recent regulations' benefits and costs—based on the government's own numbers—suggests that the goal has been excessively stringent in some cases. In chapter 3, for example, I estimate that the net benefits of regulation could increase by over $280 billion if agencies rejected regulations that do not pass a neutral economist's benefit-cost test.

This book is about domestic and international regulatory reform. It has three objectives: first, to provide an overview of regulation and its reform around the world; second, to examine what we know about the government's assessment of the benefits and costs of regulation—using the United States as an example; and, third, to explore future directions in regulation and its reform.

Chapter 2 provides an overview of regulation and its reform around the world. It examines the definition of and rationale for regulation, the benefits and costs of regulation, the impacts of major regulatory reforms, and current trends in reform. The review of the literature on the benefits and costs demonstrates that we can use standard economic analysis to explore systematically the benefits and costs of regulatory activity. Relatively good data exist on the benefits and costs of regulation in the United States, but outside the United States such data are limited. Throughout the world, a great deal of reform is taking place in economic deregulation and privatization. For the most part, such reforms appear to have led to substantial gains for consumers. While economic regulation is changing to allow for more competition among firms, social regulation appears to be increasing. A review of economic and social regulation in different countries reveals that the kind and extent of such regulation vary greatly by country. Because of the increasing concern with the impacts of regulation, a variety of oversight mechanisms and institutions are emerging to address those issues in both developed and developing countries.

In chapter 3 I provide the most comprehensive assessment to date of the costs and benefits of U.S. federal regulation. The database I developed for the analysis is based on the government's own numbers and is the most extensive available. I draw four significant conclusions from the analysis. First, the net benefits of regulations from 1981 to mid-1996 are positive. Second, many regulations would not pass a neutral economist's benefit-cost test. Third, the quality of agency analyses of regulation is generally poor, and the results of the analyses are therefore not often useful for improving regulatory outcomes. Fourth, Congress and the White House must cooperate to enforce economic analysis requirements that already exist if those branches of government are serious about reforming regulation. Successful enforcement requires high-level political support, statutory language requiring all agencies to adhere to established principles of economic analysis, and rigorous review of agency analyses by an independent entity. In chapter 3 I also offer some principles and suggestions for reforming the regulatory process.

In chapter 4 I examine the future of regulatory reform both in the United States and abroad. I argue that regulation and regulatory reform are becoming "internationalized." The internationalization of regulation has two dimensions—first, some common features exist in the nature of regulatory reforms taking place in different countries around the world. Second, regulation in areas such as the environment, labor, and finance is increasingly likely to be subject to oversight by international bodies. I argue that the forces of globalization, increases in average wealth, and our growing understanding of the impacts of regulation can help provide important clues about the future of the institution.

Regulation is likely to change dramatically in the years ahead. In the future, we are likely to see more economic deregulation and more social regulation, but the nature of social regulation is likely to undergo some dramatic changes. The increase in economic deregulation is likely to be good for the average citizen, while the changes in social regulation will have advantages and disadvantages. In general, regulation's efficacy will increase as human beings learn to develop regulatory institutions that are better suited to economic and social needs. The news is not all good from an economic standpoint, but the general direction of change is quite positive.

2

Regulation and Its Reform
around the World

During the past two decades, the developed countries have witnessed an unparalleled rise in new regulations related to the environment, health, and safety. In addition, businesses in many countries face an increasing array of demands related to paperwork and are providing such additional benefits for employees as child care and health care. During that period, many of the developed countries' industries—including airlines, trucking, railroads, financial markets, energy, and telecommunications—have undergone substantial economic deregulation. At the same time, developing countries, complementing their far-reaching privatization programs, are deregulating various sectors of the economy and devising new regulatory frameworks for others.

Analysts continue the heated debate about the effect of regulatory activity on countries' economies. While few would deny that regulation can increase consumer welfare, that outcome depends on how regulation is designed and implemented as well as on the specific problem regulation is attempting to solve. Moreover, regulation can add substantially to the costs of doing business, and firms frequently pass on those costs to consumers in the form of higher prices.

The primary contribution of this chapter is a synthesis of the growing body of literature on the effects of regulation and its reform around the world. The objective is to sketch a picture that will help provide a road map for the kinds of changes we can expect to see in the future.[1] In addition, this chapter provides some insights into how the character of regulation differs from country to country. First, I define regulation and explain its justification as well as the root causes of its inefficiencies. Then, I review the literature on the aggregate costs and benefits of regulation.[2] After examining historical trends in economic deregulation, I consider some trends in social regulation and assess recent attempts to reform the regulatory process. Finally, I present the key findings of the analysis.

The Definition of, Rationale for, and Problems with Regulation

To classify the many types of regulation, analysts traditionally assign them to the categories of economic, social, or process regulation. *Economic regulation* refers to restrictions on prices, quantity, entry, and exit for specific industries. *Social regulation* refers to regulations ostensibly aimed at correcting market imperfections that affect a wide array of industries. Typically, environmental, public health, and safety regulation fall in that category; but the category should also include mandates on employers to provide employees with benefits such as child care, medical care, and parental leave. Finally, *process regulation* refers to governmental management of the operation of the public and private sectors that imposes expensive paperwork requirements and administrative costs on both producers and consumers.

Those categories of regulation are not so neat and tidy as they might first appear. In particular, process regulation is really an integral part of much economic and social regulation. Paperwork requirements, for example, might be a significant component of such social regulation as environmental protection or worker safety. Moreover, regulations affecting education and social services do not fit neatly into any particular category. Labor regulations may affect both price and entry into the labor market, for example, by establishing a minimum wage or overtime rules. Labor regulations may also affect safety, for example, by requiring workers to wear goggles. Despite those classificatory deficiencies, assigning regulation to one of the three categories is a useful starting point for measuring many of the most important costs and benefits of regulation.

Several economic arguments support regulation.[3] The most common ones deal with correcting for market failure or ensuring distributional equity. As just suggested, a primary rationale for social regulation is that individual companies may not take responsibility for the full social cost of their actions without government intervention. For example, a firm may tend to pollute excessively unless it incurs some implicit or explicit cost for doing so. In the case of workplace safety, workers may not have sufficient information on hazards to make fully informed choices. Direct regulation represents one approach to the problem of obtaining such information.

A primary rationale for economic regulation relates to the potential for improving the efficiency of production. If economies of scale or scope exist, a single firm may, in theory, be able to produce more efficiently than several competing firms, but then the state may need to restrain that firm's monopolistic power through regulation. In addition, consumers may gain additional value as more of them use a network, as is the case in telecommunications.[4] Another rationale for economic regulation relates to the disclosure of information that may boost the confidence of investors in equity markets. That is often defined as a type of social regulation, because bank runs are a type of externality. Finally, a rationale for regulation of financial institutions such as banks exists when the costs of a bank failure can cause a general loss in confidence in the financial system. In that case, the social costs of the bank failure exceed the private costs. While we can provide some economic rationales for regulating a wide range of economic activity, such rationales are often not persuasive in practice, because government failure is just as likely as market failure.

Regulation often is inefficient, however, for both economic and political reasons. The economic reason is that a government authority has difficulty regulating companies because it lacks the necessary information. For example, a business might have a good idea of its cost and demand structure, but a regulator typically has imperfect access to such information. The firm usually is better informed than the regulator; moreover, the firm rarely has an incentive to tell the regulator all that it knows. Such informational asymmetries imply that economic regulation will rarely achieve a first-best or efficient outcome. That does not mean that regulation is not a useful approach for increasing economic efficiency when an industry is subject to increasing returns to scale or when network externalities exist. It does, however, mean that regulation has limited effectiveness and some serious structural defects. We need to keep those defects in mind when comparing that approach with viable alternatives.

Similarly, the regulator imposing social regulation must frequently base decisions on very limited information.[5] For example, in setting the total emission limitation for acid rain, the U.S. government had some crude estimates of the costs and benefits. After the program was implemented, however, the costs of achieving the emission standard were lower than expected because of the flexibility inherent in the market-based regulatory approach that the government adopted. Unforeseen changes in energy and transportation markets also played an important role.

Political problems with regulation also lead to inefficient economic results. Since regulation redistributes resources and rents, politicians often use it to secure political gains rather than to correct market failures. Politicians use a large array of regulatory instruments, such as quotas, licenses, and subsidies, to transfer significant amounts of wealth from consumers to small groups of producers. Thus, regulation often turns out to be inefficient. Classic examples arise in U.S. agriculture—special support programs for peanut, sugar, and dairy farming. Moreover, wealth transfers result from social regulation. For example, the attempts in the 1977 Clean Air Act Amendments to save high-sulfur coal mining jobs gave coal miners an implicit subsidy of $320,000 per job saved, more than twelve times their average salary.[6] When transfers are so large, beneficiaries will be willing to expend considerable resources on lobbying and other activities to enhance their earnings and protect those transfers, even when those transfers impose huge efficiency costs on the economy as a whole.

The Benefits and Costs of Regulation

Most systematic economic studies of the aggregate effects of regulation have focused on federal regulation in the United States.[7] Hahn and Hird conducted the first study to synthesize data on the benefits and costs of all federal regulation.[8] The authors estimated the annual cost of economic regulation in the United States in 1988 at approximately $45 billion in 1988 dollars and the economic transfers associated with those regulations at $170 billion to $210 billion. The authors found that the annual costs of social regulation—with a best estimate of $93 billion—were roughly comparable to annual monetized benefits—with a best estimate of $94 billion.[9]

The Hahn and Hird study demonstrated four key ideas. First, standard economic analytical techniques permit systematic assessments of the costs and benefits of regulatory activity. Second, the efficiency costs of economic regulation appear to be much smaller than the costs associated with transfers, for example, between producers and consumers. Third, such information can be useful in better understanding the economic impacts of regulation. Fourth, the data have a great deal of uncertainty.

Focusing on the cost side of regulation, Hopkins[10] extended the work of Hahn and Hird to estimate total regulatory costs in the United States at $542 billion (1991 dollars) in 1991.[11] That total accounts for over 9 percent of the gross domestic product. Hopkins's principal insight is that the costs of process regulation—expenditures related to government paperwork requirements—are substantial; they account for $189 billion of the total regulatory burden. He attributes over 80 percent of those process costs to tax paperwork. The tax compliance costs do not necessarily represent efficiency costs, however, since one must consider all aspects of a tax system to evaluate its impact on efficiency.[12] Nonetheless, the sheer magnitude of the process costs suggests that we could dramatically reduce paperwork while simultaneously improving the efficiency of the tax system.

To place the numbers in context, each American household would pay about $5,700 (1991 dollars) annually in addition to its current taxes if the government directly collected the regulatory compliance costs instead of having Americans incur them in the form of higher prices and lower wages. From another perspective, total federal spending in 1991 was about $1,200 billion— approximately twice the total cost of regulation. That two-to-one ratio between government spending and regulatory costs does not correspond to the relative emphasis each receives in either the government's statistics or its decisionmaking.

Winston updated the work on the benefits from economic deregulation in the United States.[13] Aggregate welfare gains in such sectors as airlines, railways, and road freight amounted to $35 billion to $46 billion (1990 dollars) per year.[14] Winston estimated that additional gains from remaining distortions could exceed $20 billion per year. Moreover, he subsequently argued that the estimated benefits of economic deregulation were likely to have been substantially underestimated.[15] While industry may quickly adjust prices to reflect marginal costs after deregulation, it takes time to optimize production and distribution. Frequently, analysts do not incorporate the positive effect that deregulation has on innovation when they estimate the potential gains from deregulating.

As in the case of deregulating specific industries, research suggests that we may derive substantial gains from reforming social regulation. For example, we have ample evidence that we could save more lives at a much lower cost if we reallocated resources appropriately.[16] In addition, Anderson and his colleagues estimated the savings from using market incentives in environmental regulation at $8 billion (1986 dollars) in 1992, and projected potential savings in 2000 could be as high as $38 billion, or 26 percent of estimated compliance costs.[17] Finally, in reviewing the benefits and costs of recent U.S. environmental, health, and safety regulations on the basis of the government's analyses, Hahn found that while aggregate net benefits were positive, over half the final rules would not pass a benefit-cost test.[18] Eliminating final rules that would not pass such a test could increase the present value of net benefits by more than $115 billion.[19]

We should note two points about those regulatory cost estimates, because they are often cited without careful analysis. First, the figures are highly uncertain and often incomplete.[20] Yet estimates as reported in the press and even scholarly papers sometimes fail to reflect that uncertainty. Second, the estimates are likely to understate the total impact of regulatory costs because they do not typically include the adverse effects of regulation on innovation, investment, and long-term economic growth.[21]

Turning to international comparisons, I find that the data on aggregate costs and benefits are not so complete as they are for the United States. Nonetheless, table 2-1 highlights estimates of the costs of regulation as well as the projected benefits of economic deregulation from member countries of the Organization for Economic Cooperation and Development. The numbers are shown as a percentage of GDP. Although large uncertainties are associated with the estimates,[22] the cost of regulation as a fraction of GDP is fairly significant for countries where such estimates are readily available; they range from 7 percent to 19 percent. Although we do not include data in the table relating to developing countries, some of those countries are beginning to collect information on regulatory costs. For example, one study has estimated the annual costs of selected regulations in Argentina at over $4 billion (1990 dollars).[23]

The table also reveals that nations have significant potential to achieve benefits from deregulating specific industries. Japan, Australia, and selected countries in Europe could realize benefits from deregulation on the order of 5 percent of GDP or more.[24] In comparison with measures taken to estimate welfare gains from past deregulation in the United States, analysts have made little effort to quantify such welfare gains in other countries.[25] Numerous studies have, however, assessed the gains of deregulation in both developed and developing countries by using such measures as productivity improvements or price reductions.[26] Evans and his colleagues estimated the total annual gain from productivity and pricing improvements resulting from deregulation of the telecommunications industry in New Zealand at NZ$575 million (1987 dollars).[27] Others have documented similar savings for specific industries outside the United States.[28]

Some information is available on the costs of environmental regulation outside the United States, but relatively little on the costs of other social regulation. Figure 2-1 shows how pollution abatement and control expenditures have varied as a percentage of GDP across OECD countries.[29] Those expenditures generally represent administrative costs to governments and direct control costs to the private sector. Costs range between a fraction of a percent to 2 percent of GDP.

Some caveats about the data are worth noting. First, not all pollution-abatement expenditures are directly attributable to regulation. For example, U.S. figures typically include sanitation services, which we may more properly regard as a public health service. In addition, some amount of pollution abatement spending would take place in the absence of regulation. Second, the data across countries are not directly comparable because of differences in coverage, data collection, and estimation methodology.[30]

Table 2-1 Costs of Regulation and Projected Benefits of Deregulation as a Percentage of GDP

Country	Cost of Regulation (%)	Projected Benefits of Further Economic Deregulation (%)[a]	Source
United States	7.2–9.5	.3	Hopkins (1992)[b]; Winston (1993)[c]
Australia	9–19	5.5	OECD (1996a)[d]; Belconnen Industry Commission (1995)[e]
Canada	11.8		Mihlar (1996)[f]
Japan		2.3–18.7	OECD (1997a)[g]
European Union		4.5–7	Emerson et al. (1992)[h]
Germany		.3	Lipschitz et al. (1989)[i]
Netherlands		.5–1.1	OECD (1997b)[j]

a. The projected benefits of deregulation are underestimates because the studies do not include all sectors where deregulation can be beneficial.
b. The cost estimates, as of 1991, include process costs. The range reflects the inclusion of economic transfers.
c. Winston estimated the gains of deregulation in the United States at .7–.8 percent of GDP in 1990. The .3 percent estimate represents the potential gains if the industries could achieve optimality.
d. The study derived the costs of regulation, as of 1986, from Australia (1986).
e. The study based projections of savings from deregulation on both the Hilmer and related reforms. Those reforms essentially cover legislative and regulatory changes to provide a national competition policy framework and to broaden the coverage of competition policy instruments. They also reflect moves to foster competition in national infrastructure areas such as electricity, gas, water, and road transport. The study estimated results by using a large-scale, multisectoral model of the Australian economy. The timing of the effects is unclear.
f. The author calculated cost estimates in 1993 and 1994. On the basis of an assumed ratio between private compliance costs and regulatory program spending, the author extrapolated national regulatory costs from federal and provincial administrative budgets. While the calculation is crude, it provides a rough estimate of the size of the regulatory burden.
g. The study based projections of savings from deregulation on reducing the price and productivity gap with the United States.
h. The authors based projections of savings from deregulation on dismantling technical trade barriers and custom formalities, enhanced economies of scale, and lower profit margins from enhanced competition. Using both a microeconomic and a macroeconomic model, the authors found similar results. The larger part of the effects might take five or possibly more years to be reached.
i. The authors based projections of savings from deregulation in 1990 and 1991 on more market-oriented pricing in agriculture and mining, the dismantling of tariff and nontariff barriers in selected industries, and reforms in product and labor markets. The authors combined a dynamic, macroeconomic model and a comparative-static, multisector, microeconomic model of the German economy.
j. The study cited Van Sinderen et al. (1994) and Van Bereijk and Haffner (1995). The study based projections of savings from deregulation on the reduction of product-market rigidities in twenty major sectors of the Dutch economy.

Figure 2-1 **Pollution Abatement and Control Expenditures as a Percentage of GDP**

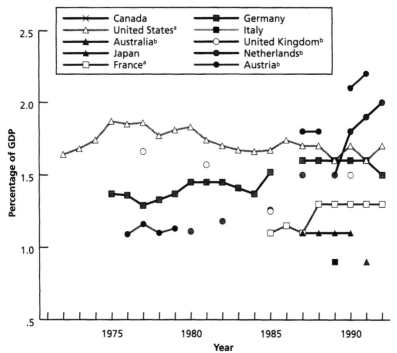

a. Expenditures by private households are included since 1972.
b. Expenditures by private households are included since 1987.

To summarize, we need a great deal more study to get a good picture of the aggregate and individual economic impacts of regulations, particularly outside the United States. At the same time, knowledge of the economic impacts of regulation has increased substantially over the past twenty-five years,[31] and that knowledge base will continue to increase throughout the world.[32] Nonetheless, in comparison with our understanding of budgets and their impacts, analysts, policymakers, and citizens have a relatively poor understanding of how regulations affect the public and private sectors.

Trends in Economic Regulation and Privatization

Analysts do not always include privatization in measures of deregulation, but that process is frequently a logical first step in deregulating an industry. Hence, I consider it here, especially for developing countries.

Figures 2-2 through 2-4 provide a useful picture of changes in the nature of domestic regulation for selected OECD countries.[33] The regulated industries include airlines, road transport, telecommunications, postal services, and utilities.[34] On the basis of the OECD's categorization of regula-

Figure 2-2 Privatization in OECD Countries

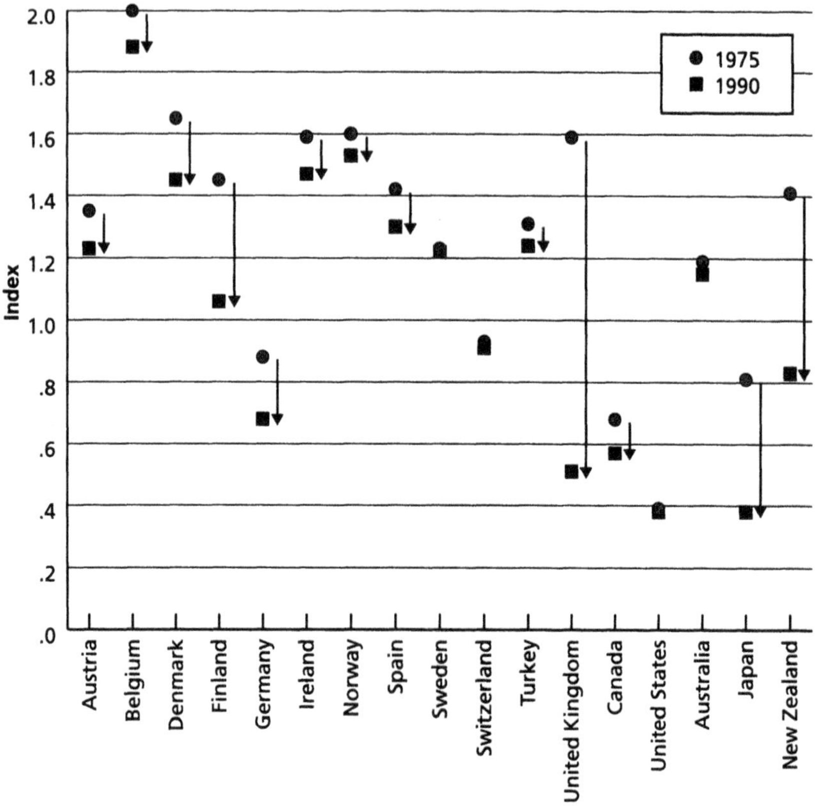

Notes: Industries include airlines, road transport, telecommunications, postal services, and utilities. The classification of regulatory status is based on a scoring system ranging from 0 (unregulated or private ownership) to 2 (highly regulated or public ownership). See OECD (1992) for a more detailed description of the scoring. The numbers correspond to the range presented on the vertical axis of the figure. The industries are weighted by their relative contribution to U.S. GDP in 1985.

tory status, I have plotted the degrees of public ownership and government control of entry and prices for the years 1975 and 1990.[35] Downward movements indicate less state ownership or control. Arrows highlight the direction of change, while their size approximates the magnitude of change. The indexes point to two trends. First, deregulation and privatization are occurring throughout the developed world. Second, the trend is especially apparent in the United States, the United Kingdom, Australia, New Zealand, and Canada, which are among the least regulated economies in the world.

That analysis has limitations, however. First, some important sectors undergoing major regulatory reform are excluded, most notably financial services and the retail sector.[36] But including those sectors would probably not change the general conclusion about the direction of reform. Second, while comparisons within countries may be reasonable, comparisons across

Figure 2-3   Deregulation of Entry Restrictions in OECD Countries

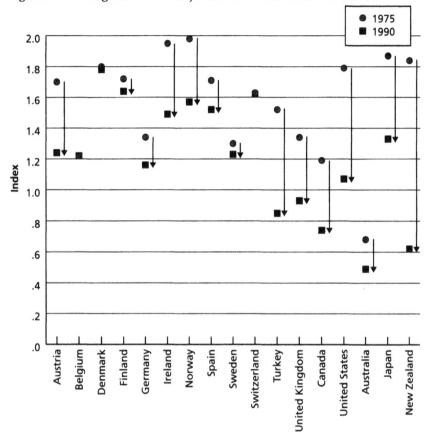

Notes: Industries include airlines, road transport, telecommunications, postal services, and utilities. The classification of regulatory status is based on a scoring system ranging from 0 (unregulated or private ownership) to 2 (highly regulated or public ownership). See OECD (1992) for a more detailed description of the scoring. The numbers correspond to the range presented on the vertical axis of the figure. The industries are weighted by their relative contribution to U.S. GDP in 1985.

countries are difficult to make on the basis of those data.[37] Finally, the data compare changes between 1975 and 1990, and many reforms have taken place since that time. Nevertheless, most of the reforms tend to be in the direction of liberalizing price and entry restrictions and promoting privatization.

Moreover, figures 2-2 through 2-4 do not provide insight into how regulatory reforms spread throughout the world. Although that subject is difficult to characterize, a preliminary review of the data suggests that in many of the industries included in the figures, such as airlines, road freight, and telecommunications, the United States was the first or among the first to initiate major reforms, beginning in the late 1970s and the mid-1980s. Liberalization of those industries—including substantial privatization—fol-

Figure 2-4 Deregulation of Price Restrictions in OECD Countries

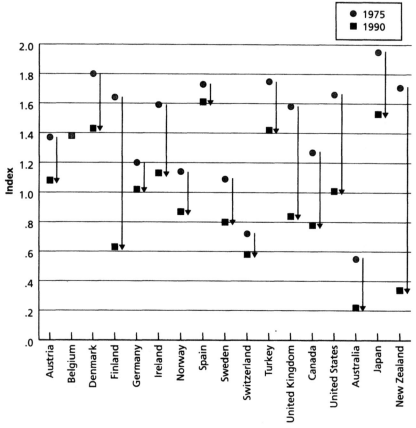

Notes: Industries include airlines, road transport, telecommunications, postal services, and utilities. The classification of regulatory status is based on a scoring system ranging from 0 (unregulated or private ownership) to 2 (highly regulated or public ownership). See OECD (1992) for a more detailed description of the scoring. The numbers correspond to the range presented on the vertical axis of the figure. The industries are weighted by their relative contribution to U.S. GDP in 1985.

lowed in other OECD countries, including Australia, Canada, New Zealand, and the United Kingdom, throughout the rest of the 1980s. Reform tended to move more slowly throughout Japan and continental Europe.[38] Certainly, exceptions to the generalization described above exist. For example, road freight was substantially deregulated in Australia, Sweden, Switzerland, and the United Kingdom in the 1950s and 1960s. In 1985 Japan was among the first countries to deregulate its telecommunications sector substantially, as the government partially privatized Nippon Telegraph and Telephone, abolished its monopoly position, and allowed competition in network activities. In such industries as utilities and bus services, that pattern does not hold or, at least, is not so apparent.

Figure 2-5 Ownership of Service Industries in Developing Countries

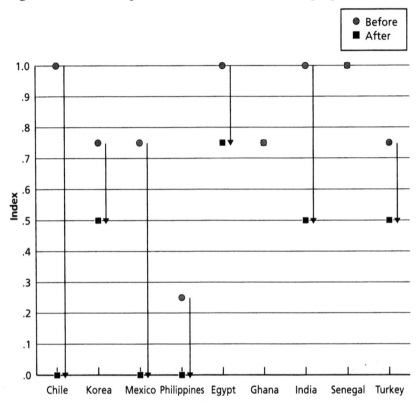

Notes: Service-sector industries include airlines, urban transports, telecommunications, and ports. The classification of regulatory status is based on a scoring system ranging from 0 (low government control/open markets or private ownership) to 1 (high government control/closed markets or public ownership) adapted by the author from World Bank (1995). In general, any categorization not classified as a "state-owned monopoly" was considered to be privately owned. Likewise, any categorization not classified as either "no monopoly" or "free prices" was considered to be associated with high government control/closed markets. The numbers correspond to the range presented on the vertical axis of the figure.

Figures 2-5 through 2-8 show the status of domestic competition before and after major efforts at reform and provide a perspective on selected developing countries. I base the scoring, not directly comparable to that in figures 2-2 through 2-4, on a relatively crude categorization of the nature of state ownership and level of competition in several product and service industries.[39] Downward movements indicate a more open and competitive market. Like figures 2-2 through 2-4, figures 2-5 through 2-8 highlight trends instead of providing absolute rankings among countries. The key point is that both privatization and deregulation are opening markets in many developing countries.[40] The economic success of those reform initiatives varies widely.[41]

Figure 2-6 Regulation of Service Industries in Developing Countries

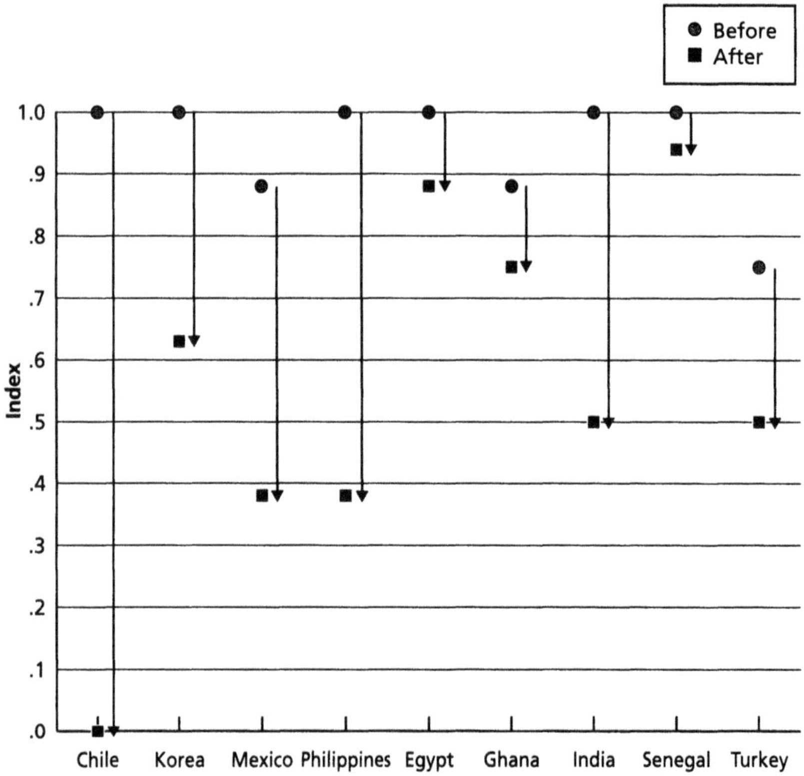

Notes: Service-sector industries include airlines, urban transports, telecommunications, and ports. The classification of regulatory status is based on a scoring system ranging from 0 (low government control/open markets or private ownership) to 1 (high government control/closed markets or public ownership) adapted by the author from World Bank (1995). In general, any categorization not classified as a "state-owned monopoly" was considered to be privately owned. Likewise, any categorization not classified as either "no monopoly" or "free prices" was considered to be associated with high government control/closed markets. The numbers correspond to the range presented on the vertical axis of the figure.

In addition to changes in the regulation of specific economic sectors, the regulation of labor markets differs substantially across countries. Many authors have tried to characterize the nature of labor regulation. In an early comprehensive study, Grubb and Wells ranked European Community countries on the basis of the strictness of employment legislation, including such measures as restrictions on employers' freedom to dismiss workers, restrictions on work hours, and limits on employers' use of temporary labor.[42] Their rankings indicate that some north European countries, such as the United Kingdom, Denmark, and Ireland, were the least regulated among the European Community, while some south European countries, such as Spain and Greece, were the most regulated. The OECD extended that work

Figure 2-7 Ownership of Product Industries in Developing Countries

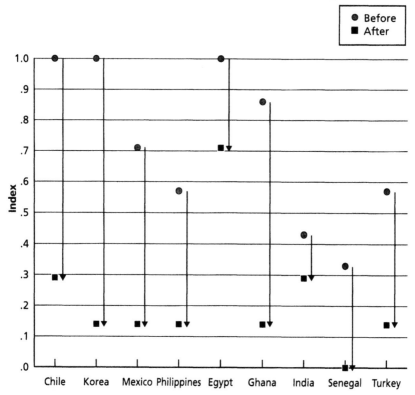

Notes: Product-sector industries include petroleum, fertilizer, mining, sugar, textiles, cement, and steel. The classification of regulatory status is based on a scoring system ranging from 0 (low government control/open markets or private ownership) to 1 (high government control/closed markets or public ownership) adapted by the author from World Bank (1995). In general, any categorization not classified as a "state-owned monopoly" was considered to be privately owned. Likewise, any categorization not classified as either "no monopoly" or "free prices" was considered to be associated with high government control/closed markets. The numbers correspond to the range presented on the vertical axis of the figure.

to include non-European OECD countries and found that the United States, Canada, Australia, the United Kingdom, and New Zealand had some of the most flexible employment legislation in the world.[43]

Although those rankings are illustrative, we should interpret them carefully. First, the selection, measurement, and weighing of the determinants of labor regulation are often quite subjective.[44] Second, regulation only partially determines the degree of flexibility in labor markets. Other important factors include cultural norms, such as Japan's long-term employment model, and legal systems that establish the nature of collective bargaining. Nonetheless, observers have noted that labor market regulations in many European countries are more restrictive than in the United States[45] and

Figure 2-8 Regulation of Product Industries in Developing Countries

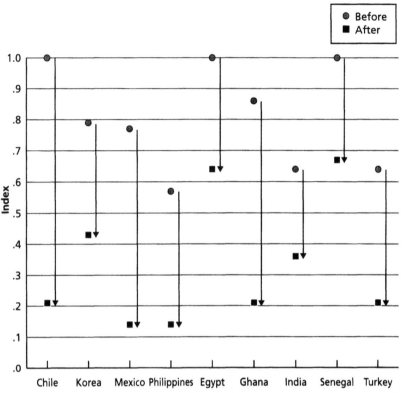

Notes: Product-sector industries include petroleum, fertilizer, mining, sugar, textiles, cement, and steel. The classification of regulatory status is based on a scoring system ranging from 0 (low government control/open markets or private ownership) to 1 (high government control/closed markets or public ownership) adapted by the author from World Bank (1995). In general, any categorization not classified as a "state-owned monopoly" was considered to be privately owned. Likewise, any categorization not classified as either "no monopoly" or "free prices" was considered to be associated with high government control/closed markets. The numbers correspond to the range presented on the vertical axis of the figure.

that labor market flexibility is an important contributing factor to growth, productivity, and employment.[46]

Measuring the direction of change in labor market regulation throughout the world is difficult. While such regulation remains quite onerous in many European countries, some pressure is mounting to allow more flexibility in labor markets because of current economic problems. In addition, one justification of the move toward a common European currency is that it will force governments to liberalize their labor roles. Ironically, just as Europe may be recognizing the need to reduce its labor regulation, the United States has seen its labor market subjected to more regulation, principally through increased legislation associated with mandating employee benefits such as child and health care.[47]

The pace and the level of regulatory reform vary greatly around the world. In addition, different countries have applied different approaches to reform.[48] Nonetheless, this overview of economic regulation and privatization reveals that those activities are moving forward in developed and developing countries. Analysts are beginning to document the impact of those changes on economic well-being; the general results suggest a positive correlation between less economic regulation and improved economic well-being.

Trends in Social Regulation

By most measures, social regulation in developed countries appears to have increased rapidly in the 1980s and to have continued to grow during the 1990s.[49] Unfortunately, measures of regulatory growth, including the size of regulatory agencies, the number of rules promulgated, or the number of pages in a code of regulations, are relatively crude because they are unlikely to be closely correlated with the net benefits of regulation. In addition, limited information on the benefits and costs of regulatory requirements exists outside the United States. Within the United States, Hopkins has shown that the annualized costs of social regulation, comprising primarily environmental costs, have grown in real terms since the late 1970s,[50] and the substantial costs of new requirements suggest that the total burden will continue to increase.[51] Moreover, figure 2-1 provides some evidence that environmental expenditures in developed countries are increasing in real terms at a rate comparable to or slightly greater than GDP.[52] No similar data exist for developing countries.

It is inappropriate to examine the costs of social regulation without considering the associated benefits. Information on the net benefits of regulations over time is quite limited, however. While data do not exist outside the United States, several countries have begun to assess the benefits and costs of individual regulations.[53]

The trends in the total net benefits of social regulation are not readily apparent. For example, in my comprehensive examinations of recent major environmental, health, and safety regulations in the United States, I was unable to discern a distinct pattern for how the net benefits of individual regulations have varied over time.[54] Nevertheless, a trend toward using nontraditional approaches to regulating health, safety, and the environment is evident.[55] Examples include performance standards, dissemination of information on risks, labeling, recycling, and the use of markets for environmental protection. In addition, interest is growing in designing more cost-effective regulatory approaches.

In conclusion, social regulation appears to be on the rise throughout the developed world, but measures are often crude. Limited information on costs exists outside the United States. Furthermore, a lack of data makes it difficult to assess the net benefits of social regulation. Finally, we see a trend toward using alternative approaches to regulation that attempt to achieve better social outcomes at a lower social cost.

Recent Attempts at Reforming the Regulatory Process

It is useful now to examine in detail the carefully documented attempts at reforming the regulatory process around the world. Table 2-2 provides an overview of regulatory reforms in several countries. The first column notes whether the oversight mechanism is a permanent feature in government, while the second column identifies the extent to which governments have reviewed existing regulatory activities and procedures. I categorize the review processes as either "ad hoc/one-time" or "continuous" to reflect the degree to which the process is institutionalized.[56] The last columns describe the analytical requirements for new regulatory activities. The table highlights the initiation of reform, the type of analysis required, and any decision criteria.

While simple categorizations gloss over significant variations in policies among countries, the table shows that regulatory oversight is an important issue in OECD countries.[57] Indeed, all those countries have some requirements for the review of existing rules, the analysis of new rules, or both. Several countries require benefit-cost analysis of new laws or regulations, while others require at least some analysis of costs. Although the coverage of activities and the scope of authority vary among countries, regulators generally prepare the analyses—often with oversight or guidance from another government agency or institution.[58] Only in a few cases are strict economic criteria employed, such as the requirement that benefits justify costs.

Table 2-3 highlights past accomplishments and projected benefits of review efforts in selected countries. Measures of the success of such reviews, which include the number of rules reviewed or eliminated, streamlined procedures, and cost savings, are highlighted in the second column. While some of the results are impressive, in many cases evaluating their actual economic impact is difficult. For example, simply reducing the number of rules may not result in any real savings if the rules eliminated are outdated and no longer enforced. Comprehensive measurement of impacts will always be difficult, and more resources are likely to be required to

Table 2-2 Overview of Regulatory Reform Efforts around the World

Country or State	Oversight of Regulatory Reform[a]	Review of Existing Activities[b]	Initiated	Analysis of New Activities	
				Analysis Requirements	Decision Criteria
Australia	Permanent	Continuous	1985	Benefit-cost analysis	
New South Wales	Permanent	Continuous	1989	Benefit-cost analysis or cost-effectiveness analysis	Benefit-cost and cost-effectiveness test preferred
Queensland	Permanent	Continuous	1990; revised 1995	Benefit-cost analysis	Benefit-cost test preferred
Victoria	Permanent	Continuous	1984	Benefit-cost analysis	
Austria	None	None	1992	Fiscal analysis recommended	
Canada	Permanent	One-time	1977; revised 1986, 1992	Benefit-cost analysis or cost-effectiveness analysis; more complex analysis required for rules with present value over CAN$50 million	
Finland	Ad hoc	One-time	1970s; revised 1990	General impact analysis	
Germany	Ad hoc	One-time	1984; revised 1989	Not mandatory; benefit-cost analysis suggested	
Iceland	None	None	Proposed 1995	General impact/fiscal analysis proposed	
Japan	Ad hoc	One-time	1987; revised 1988	General impact analysis as considered necessary by regulators	
Mexico	Permanent	One-time	1996	Benefit-cost analysis	
Netherlands	Permanent	Continuous	1985	General impact analysis	
New Zealand	Permanent	One-time	1996	Fiscal analysis	
Norway	Ad hoc	One-time	1985; revised 1995	Consequence (fiscal) analysis; benefit-cost analysis recommended as appropriate	
Portugal	Ad hoc	One-time	n.a.	Fiscal analysis	
Sweden	Permanent	One-time	1987; revised 1994	Consequence/distributional/fiscal analysis; includes benefit-cost analysis and cost-effectiveness analysis for rules with significant negative effects	
United Kingdom	Permanent	One-time	1985; revised 1995	Benefit-cost analysis	
United States	Permanent	One-time	1974; revised 1977, 1981, 1993, 1995	Benefit-cost analysis; more complex analysis required for "economically significant" rules	Cost-effectiveness test unless otherwise required by law

a. Permanent indicates that an agency or unit is involved in regulatory administration. Ad hoc indicates that a temporary commission or task force exists.
b. Continuous indicates that reviews are institutionalized on an ongoing basis. One-time indicates singular or occasional review(s).
Sources: OECD (1997b) and Mexico (1997).

23

Table 2-3 Review of Existing Regulatory Activities and Procedures

Country or State	Background	Selected Results
Australia	A systematic review of all regulations initiated by the Competition Principles Agreement in 1995. By 2000, all existing regulations that restrict competition must be reformed unless demonstrated to be in the public interest. Previously, review was done on an ad hoc basis.	The repeal of outdated regulations is part of the more comprehensive Hilmer reforms that are expected to yield annual gains in real GDP of 5.5 percent, or A$23 billion per year, when fully implemented (Belconnen Industry Commission 1995).
New South Wales	In 1989 a staged repeal of all existing regulations began that built on earlier efforts of the mid-1980s. A permanent sunset program (seven years) was adopted in 1989 (OECD 1996a).	The stock of rules made before 1990 was reduced from 976 to 646, a one-third drop (OECD 1996a).
Queensland	A systematic review of all laws and lower-level regulations, overseen by the Business Regulatory Review Unit, was completed from 1991 to 1995. That built on less formal review efforts of the late 1980s. A permanent sunset program (ten years) was adopted in 1995 (OECD 1996a).	Net cost savings for businesses were estimated at over A$370 million a year, and savings to consumers were substantially higher (OECD 1996a).
Victoria	The Office of Regulatory Reform carried out a systematic review of entire regulatory structures from 1987 to 1990. A permanent sunset program (ten years) was adopted in 1984 (OECD 1996a).	Total savings from the repeal program were estimated at between A$140 million and A$200 million a year (OECD 1996a).
Canada	Regulatory departments completed a one-time review of twenty-six federal departments and agencies in 1993. In 1994 a detailed review of regulations in six key sectors was initiated (OECD 1997b).	As of 1993, 835 rules were revised or eliminated (OECD 1997b).
Mexico	The Economic Deregulation Unit is completing a systematic review of business formalities, initiated by the Agreement for the Deregulation of Business in 1995.	Over 30 percent of all business formalities have been reviewed to date, and 80 percent were expected to be reviewed by the end of 1997. A substantial number were eliminated or simplified (Mexico 1997). In Mexico City over 30 percent of business formalities have been eliminated, and 75 percent must be processed in under ten working days. In addition, the time required for new business approvals has been greatly reduced (Mexico 1997).
Sweden	A one-time review of regulations was initiated in the 1980s under the "guillotine" rule (OECD 1997b).	Hundreds of regulations that were not centrally registered were nullified (OECD 1997b).
United Kingdom	The Deregulation Initiative instituted a systematic review of all laws that is overseen by the Deregulation Task Force.	By the end of 1996, over 1,000 regulations were repealed or amended (Avery 1997). In addition, forty-eight deregulatory orders changing primary legislation have saved over £100 million annually (Avery 1997).
United States	Legislation, executive orders, and executive programs initiated various one-time reviews of selected regulations.	As a result of President Bush's regulatory review and agency moratorium in 1992, it was estimated that $15 billion to $20 billion were saved from actions taken or planned during the ninety-day review (OMB 1993). President Clinton's National Performance Review proposed that regulatory agencies eliminate 16,000 pages of regulations and modify 31,000 more (Gore 1996).

account accurately for real economic savings instead of using measures that crudely approximate regulatory impacts.

The United States, the first country to establish comprehensive efforts at reform, provides a good example of some of the changes that are taking place in requirements for regulatory analysis. Tables 2-4 and 2-5 show legislation and selected executive orders aimed at reforming the regulatory process and examining the economic impacts of new and existing rules.[59]

The tables reveal several important insights. First, both Congress and the president have perceived problems with the regulatory system and have attempted to address those deficiencies through process reform. Perhaps because of the politicized nature of the debate over regulatory reform, however, those reform efforts have come about in a piecemeal fashion, and the requirements for analysis have some overlap. For example, under both the Unfunded Mandates Reform Act and Executive Order 12866, executive branch agencies must prepare benefit-cost analyses for major rules. Second, the major aims of the efforts to date have been to require more information on the benefits and costs of regulations and to increase the oversight of regulatory activities and agency performance.

While the efforts described in tables 2-4 and 2-5 provide a systematic way to identify and lay the groundwork for correcting regulatory shortcomings often driven by poorly designed statutes, Congress has rarely made fundamental changes in the statutes themselves. For instance, process reforms often have little effect on rules from statutes, such as the Clean Air Act, that contain provisions explicitly prohibiting the consideration of costs, benefits, or both. Table 2-6 highlights recent U.S. legislation specifically aimed at placing greater emphasis on the consideration of benefits and costs. For example, the Delaney Clause, which set a zero-tolerance standard for carcinogens from pesticide residues in processed foods, was recently repealed under the Food Quality Protection Act. Now, if a pesticide exceeds a negligible risk, regulators are allowed to consider the benefits from using the pesticide when they decide how to regulate it. In only one case, however, the Pipeline Safety and Partnership Act, is the agency actually required to show that the benefits of a rule justify its costs before the agency issues a new standard.

In addition to the efforts at the federal level, many states have recently undertaken major efforts to reform the regulatory process in the past few years. For example, in a survey of all fifty states, the National Association on Administrative Rules Review found that thirty-eight states currently have requirements in place to analyze the economic impacts of new activities.[60] Table 2-7 highlights efforts in five states. The table describes both the efforts to review existing rules and procedures, including any measures of

Table 2-4   Recent U.S. Initiatives to Review New Regulatory Activity

Authority	Description
Executive Order 12866 of 1993[a]	Requires agencies to analyze the potential benefits and costs of an "economically significant" regulatory action and submit the results to the Office of Management and Budget's Office of Information and Regulatory Affairs for review. A rule is considered economically significant if it has an annual effect on the economy of $100 million or more or significantly disrupts the economy, a sector of the economy, productivity, competition, jobs, the environment, public health or safety, or state, local, or tribal governments. Also requires agencies to assess the benefits and costs of "significant" rules, a less rigorous requirement than the requirement for economically significant rules. A rule is considered "significant" if it interferes with actions of other agencies, has significant budgetary impacts, or raises novel legal or policy issues.
Unfunded Mandates Reform Act of 1995[b]	Requires the Congressional Budget Office to estimate the direct costs of laws with new mandates in excess of $50 million in any one year on state, local, and tribal governments and in excess of $100 million in any one year on the private sector. Also requires agencies to assess the benefits and costs of regulations with new mandates in excess of $100 million in any one year on state, local, and tribal governments or the private sector. Requires the agency to choose the "least costly, most cost-effective, or least burdensome alternative" unless the provisions are inconsistent with law or the head of an agency can explain why the agency did not adopt such an alternative.
Small Business Regulatory Enforcement Fairness Act of 1996[c]	Requires agencies to submit each final regulation and supporting analyses to Congress and the General Accounting Office. Congress has at least sixty calendar days to review major regulations and can enact a joint resolution of disapproval to void the regulation if the resolution is passed and signed by the president. Strengthens judicial review provisions to hold agencies more accountable for the impacts of regulation on small entities.
Regulatory Accountability Provisions of 1996, 1997, and 1998[d]	In separate appropriations legislation in 1996, 1997, and 1998, Congress required the Office of Management and Budget to submit an assessment of the annual benefits and costs of all federal regulatory programs to Congress for 1997, 1998, and 2000, respectively.

a. This order contains similar requirements to Executive Order 12291 issued by President Reagan in 1981.
b. Public Law 104-4.
c. This provision, contained in the Contract with America Advancement Act of 1996, Public Law 104-21, §251, amends the Regulatory Flexibility Act of 1980.
d. Treasury, Postal Service, and General Government Appropriations Act, 1997, Public Law 104-208, §645; Treasury, Postal Service, and General Government Appropriations Act, 1998, Public Law 105-61, §625; and Conference Report on H.R. 4328, Making Omnibus Consolidated and Emergency Supplemental Appropriations for Fiscal Year 1999, §638.

Table 2-5 Recent U.S. Initiatives to Review Existing Regulation

Authority	Description
National Performance Review[a]	Orders agencies to conduct a page-by-page review of all regulations in the *Code of Federal Regulations* and to eliminate or modify rules in need of reform.
Telecommunications Act of 1996[b]	Requires the Federal Communications Commission to conduct a biennial review of all regulations to determine whether any of the regulations are no longer necessary as a result of "meaningful economic competition" between telecommunications service providers.
Regulatory Accountability Provisions of 1996, 1997, and 1998[c]	In separate appropriations legislation in 1996, 1997, and 1988, Congress required the Office of Management and Budget to submit an assessment of the annual benefits and costs of all federal regulatory programs to Congress for 1997, 1998, and 2000, respectively. Also allows the Office of Management and Budget to make recommendations to reform or eliminate inefficient programs.

a. Executive Memorandum to Heads of Agencies (March 4, 1995).
b. Public Law 104-104, §402.
c. Treasury, Postal Service, and General Government Appropriations Act, 1997, Public Law 104-208, §645; Treasury, Postal Service, and General Government Appropriations Act, 1998, Public Law 105-61, §625; and Conference Report on H.R. 4328, Making Omnibus Consolidated and Emergency Supplemental Appropriations for Fiscal Year 1999, §638.

Table 2-6 Recent U.S. Legislation with Greater Emphasis on Balancing Benefits and Costs

Statute	Description
Food Quality Protection Act of 1996[a]	Eliminates the Delaney Clause of the Food, Drug, and Cosmetic Act, which set a zero-tolerance standard for carcinogenic pesticide residues on processed foods. Establishes a "safe" tolerance level for residues on raw or processed foods, defined as "reasonable certainty of no harm." Allows the administrator of the Environmental Protection Agency to modify the tolerance level if use of the pesticide protects consumers from health risks greater than the dietary risk from the residue or if use is necessary to avoid a "significant disruption" of the food supply. Amends the Federal Insecticide, Fungicide, and Rodenticide Act by requiring a reevaluation of the safe tolerance level after the administrator determines during the reregistration process whether a pesticide will present an "unreasonable risk to man or the environment, taking into account the economic, social, and environmental costs and benefits of the use of any pesticide."
Safe Drinking Water Act Amendments of 1996[b]	Amends the procedure to set maximum contaminant levels for contaminants in public water supplies. Adds a requirement to determine whether the benefits of the level justify the costs. Maintains the feasibility standard for contaminant levels, unless the feasible level would result in an increase in the concentration of other contaminants or would interfere with the efficacy of treatment techniques used to comply with other national drinking water regulations. Requires the administrator of the Environmental Protection Agency to set contaminant levels to minimize the total risk of adverse health effects by balancing the risk from the contaminant and the risk from other contaminants in such cases.
Accountable Pipeline Safety and Partnership Act of 1996[c]	Requires the secretary of the Department of Transportation to consider the benefits and costs expected to result from the implementation of a safety standard and to propose a standard only if the benefits justify the costs. The benefit and cost estimates are based on a risk assessment, for which the secretary must identify regulatory and nonregulatory options and must explain the selection of the standard in lieu of other options.

a. Public Law 104-170, §§404-405.
b. Public Law 104-182, §104.
c. Public Law 104-304, §4.

success, and the analysis requirements for new activities. While the efforts vary in their authority, coverage of activities, and amount of resources, they all place greater emphasis on economic analysis and the review of existing regulations and procedures. In addition, some states have begun to document the success of their efforts; the measures have generally been limited to the number of rules reviewed or eliminated, however. Few estimates of actual welfare gains are available.

Amid growing sensitivity to the costs of regulation and the possibility of designing new approaches to regulation, governments around the world are introducing oversight mechanisms and institutions to reform the regulatory process. Most OECD countries have implemented mechanisms for reviewing existing rules and procedures or analyzing the economic impacts of new rules and activities or doing both. Similar efforts are taking place in Mexico and other developing countries. Whether those reforms have resulted in substantial economic gains is unclear. While analysts have documented positive impacts in some cases, governments will need to spend more resources to assess the effectiveness of those reforms.

Conclusions

This chapter has analyzed regulation and its reform throughout the world. The review of the literature on the benefits and costs demonstrates that we can systematically explore the benefits and costs of regulatory activity by using standard economic analysis. Poorly designed or inappropriate regulation can have a significant adverse impact on economic growth. Specifically, regulation aimed at controlling prices and entry into markets that would otherwise be workably competitive is likely to reduce the average standard of living. In addition, process regulation that is unnecessary can impose a significant cost on the economy. Nonetheless, social regulations may have significant net benefits for the average consumer. At the same time, those regulations may not effectively meet goals and in some cases may result in a net decline in living standards. That underscores the importance of conducting economic analysis that will enhance the quality of regulations.

Relatively good data exist on the benefits and costs of regulation in the United States, although they are certainly far from complete. Outside the United States, the data on costs and benefits are limited. Other OECD countries have begun to assemble some estimates of benefits and costs, but that process will take time. A few developing countries are beginning to engage in that analytical exercise as well. It is fair to say that the understanding of the impacts of regulation has increased over the past twenty-five years, and evidence suggests that the knowledge base will continue to grow. Nonethe-

Table 2-7 Overview of Regulatory Reform Efforts in Selected States

State	Initiated	Review of Existing Rules			Analysis of New Rules		
		Coverage	Examples of Results	Key Revisions[a]	Required Analysis	Requirement for Benefits to Exceed Costs
Arizona	1986	Continuous (S)	49 percent of the 1,392 rules reviewed in fiscal year 1996 were identified for modification (Malanowski 1997).	1993	Economic impact (S)	All rules (S)
California	1995	One-time (E)	3,900 regulations were identified for repeal; 1,700 were recommended for modification (Wilson 1996).	1991–1993, 1997	Economic impact (S)	Selected rules (S, E)
Massachusetts	1996	One-time (E)	Of the 1,595 regulations reviewed, 19 percent were identified for repeal and 44 percent were identified for modification (Massachusetts 1996).	1996	Economic impact (S, E)	All rules (E)
New York	1995, 1996	One-time (E), continuous (S)	n.a.	1995	Economic impact (S); benefit–cost for selected rules (E)	All rules (E)
Virginia	1994	Continuous (E)	Agencies reviewed 1,457 regulations and recommended the modification of 41 percent of rules and the elimination of 30 percent of the rules (Virginia 1997).	1994	Economic impact (S)	None

Note: The authority for review and analysis appears in parentheses. E indicates an executive order, and S indicates a statute.

a. Although many of these states previously had some requirements for analysis of new rules, the requirements resulted in cursory review. Important revisions were made through new executive orders and statutory changes to clarify and expand requirements and to establish oversight.

less, compared with measures of government budgets, measures of regulation are in their infancy.

Deregulation and privatization are moving forward in both the developed and developing world. In some countries, such as the United States and New Zealand, deregulation is further along, and the debate centers around how much deregulation is appropriate in network industries. Other developed and developing countries need to privatize or deregulate a substantial number of industries. The starting point for reform, the type of reform, and the pace of reform vary greatly across countries. Future structural changes aimed at liberalizing regulated and state-owned industries could have enormous positive impacts on country economies as well as on the global economy. Less is understood about the quantitative impact of labor market restrictions; we do, however, find growing evidence that labor market flexibility is an important contributing factor to growth, productivity, and employment.

While economic regulation is changing to allow for more competition among firms, social regulation (as measured by direct environmental costs) takes up on the order of 1 to 2 percent of GDP in many developed countries and appears to be growing, although the data are sparse. The magnitude of social regulation in developing countries is likely to be smaller but is probably growing at a more rapid rate. Whether social regulation has increased aggregate welfare is unclear. Only in the United States do we have enough data to infer rough estimates of the net benefits of social regulation. We know even less in developing countries, where many governments are only beginning to construct regulatory frameworks that address those social concerns. The growing interest in using alternative approaches to regulation that attempt to achieve better social outcomes at a lower social cost is important. Analysts have quantified the impact of some of those efforts.

We know relatively little about the benefits and costs of specific regulations, but a variety of oversight mechanisms and institutions are developing to address those issues in both developed and developing countries. Those institutions are focusing on existing regulations, new regulations, or both. The effectiveness of those efforts is likely to vary dramatically. The emerging institutions aimed at reforming social and process regulations should help furnish new insights on appropriate directions for reforming the regulatory process.

3

Regulatory Reform: Assessing the U.S. Government's Numbers

Since the political earthquake that shook Washington in November of 1994 brought with it bipartisan calls for regulatory reform, scholars and journalists have been raising the public's awareness of the unintended consequences of government regulation. Policymakers, goaded by the continuing analysis of regulatory successes and failures, have acted to redress regulation gone awry. California, for example, decided to ban the use of MTBE (methyl tertiary butyl ether), a gasoline additive used to improve air quality, when the state found that the substance posed a risk to the water supply. Congress could have avoided that outcome if the 1990 Clean Air Act Amendments had required a careful risk assessment before manufacturers introduced the substance into the gasoline supply.[1] Another problematic regulation required automobile manufacturers to install airbags, which turn out to pose serious risks to children and small passengers. Philip Howard's insightful bestseller *The Death of Common Sense* provides several other examples of regulation run amok.[2] Clearly, our regulatory system urgently requires repair.

This chapter provides the most comprehensive assessment to date of the impact of federal regulatory activities on the economy.[3] The analysis is based on a review of all rules with regulatory impact analyses, or RIAs, that I could locate from 1981 through mid-1996, a total of 168 final and proposed rules.[4] I also examined the preamble of the *Federal Register* notice for each rule; the preamble typically summarizes the information that the RIA presents.[5] I estimated the net benefits of 106 final regulations and 30 proposed regulations, calculated the cost-effectiveness of 52 final regulations, and estimated benefit-cost ratios for 105 final regulations.[6] The net benefits of final regulations approach a net present value of $1.8 trillion. Most of the benefits from final rules result from the estimated reduction in the risk of death, disease, and injury. Nonfatal benefits account for about half of that total. The remaining benefits are from air pollution reduction, the only pollution reduction benefits that agencies consistently quantify.[7] Those benefits can include health and mortality risk reduction benefits as well as other benefits, such as materials damages.

The analysis in this chapter builds on pathbreaking work done at the Office of Management and Budget beginning in the early 1980s and subsequent work by regulatory scholars.[8] Officials at the OMB ranked health, safety, and environmental regulations in terms of cost-effectiveness and found that the cost-effectiveness of regulations varies across a wide spectrum. Scholars further found that agencies are not maximizing the net benefits of regulation. My study further supports those discoveries. The results of the studies imply that agencies should reallocate resources to regulations with higher net benefits or to regulatory strategies that are more cost-effective than strategies agencies currently employ. The results also imply that we need a more consistent approach to regulatory analysis to ensure that agencies choose the best regulatory policies and programs.

Scholars have designed reform proposals that push for improving the regulatory process by strengthening executive regulatory oversight and increasing the use of economic analysis.[9] Partly as a result of those proposals, every president since Nixon, in addition to building public support for regulatory reform, has advocated a specific type of reform.[10] Because the real impact of those reform efforts is questionable, this chapter provides guidance for further reform of the regulatory process. I discuss the extent to which federal agencies have cataloged information on the benefits and costs of regulatory activities, the role of benefit-cost analysis in the regulatory process, factors affecting the efficiency of regulation, and the relationship between a statute's requirements for economic analysis and the net benefits of regulations from that statute. The study shows that further use of economic analysis and enforcement of economic analysis requirements are necessary to improve regulatory outcomes.

After assessing the quality of various agencies' estimates of the benefits and costs of regulation, I present the key analytical results concerning the net benefits of federal regulations for which an agency provided enough information to calculate net benefits. I also estimate the cost-effectiveness of selected regulations. Then, I evaluate the relationship between the wording of statutory requirements for economic analysis and the efficiency of regulations and discuss whether regulatory impact analyses have improved the regulatory process. Finally, I conclude with suggestions for further regulatory reform.

How Complete Are the Government's Numbers?

As a result of Reagan's regulatory impact analysis requirement in Executive Order 12291, agencies are providing more information about the benefits and costs of federal regulation than ever before.[11] The agency RIAs do not, however, generally adhere to established principles of benefit-cost analysis and are not subject to review by an independent entity. As a result, the information provided in RIAs tends to vary in quality and quantity by agency and by type of regulation. The evaluation of the benefits and costs of regulation is therefore more difficult than it would be if the agencies applied a consistent analytical approach. Nevertheless, many scholars have used the RIA data to evaluate the regulatory process.[12] The work of those scholars as well as the analysis presented in this chapter has generally focused on agency compliance with economic analysis requirements in the Reagan and Clinton executive orders and the quality of agencies' analyses. Scholars have found that the information provided in the RIA is often not complete and that the level of detail and analytical sophistication varies across agencies and types of regulations. Common deficiencies cited throughout much of the literature include inadequate consideration of alternatives, poor treatment of uncertainty, incomplete estimation of benefits and costs, and various methodological errors.[13] My analysis supports other regulatory scholars' findings about the quality of agency RIAs.

I find that the RIAs lack analytical consistency and that agencies only superficially comply with the requirements in the Reagan and Clinton executive orders. For example, the discount rate used by a particular agency varies across regulations, and agencies do not always indicate the year in which specified benefits and costs apply. Agencies may show such information only in some years instead of presenting full streams of benefits and costs. Perhaps most important, in many cases a particular agency did not complete its quantitative analysis of benefits or cost savings. Since the lack of quantification makes it difficult to hold agencies accountable for their decisions, I closely examine the quantification issue. I consider the Environmental Protection Agency particularly carefully because other scholars have noted that the EPA tends to quantify benefits and costs less rigorously than other agencies.

Here, I do not address whether the numbers contained in the RIAs are biased, although that is an important issue. I have argued elsewhere that because bureaucrats in agencies have an incentive to overstate benefits and understate costs, agencies are likely to overstate net benefits.[14] Rather than repeat the arguments contained in my 1996 study, I simply state that the issue requires more thorough research. Moreover, I am dubious that the issue will be resolved in a way that satisfies different interest groups. Ultimately, I believe that the solution rests on devising an institutional structure that gives agencies the incentive to provide less biased information. The focus of this study is to evaluate the government's numbers, regardless of bias.

Table 3-1 shows the number and percentage of regulations for which agencies quantified some part of benefits and costs.[15] For 98 percent of the cases, agencies reported information on costs. Agencies assessed benefits, cost savings, or both for 87 percent of the rules. The EPA and the U.S. Department of Agriculture are the only agencies that did not assess benefits, cost savings, or both for all regulations.[16] An agency's decision to quantify the benefits or cost savings of a regulation appears to depend on the specific agency and the type of regulation. Agencies addressing safety risks assess benefits more often than do agencies addressing health and environmental risks.[17] One can explain that, in part, because some environmental risks, such as those attached to ecosystem degradation, are difficult to assess.[18] Fewer agencies attempted to monetize the benefits of the rule than to assess its physical effects. While the Department of Health and Human Services, the Department of Housing and Urban Development, and the Consumer Product Safety Commission monetized benefits for all rules, agencies reported monetized benefits for only about one-fourth of all rules. A few agencies, such as the Occupational Safety and Health Administration, often highlighted significant cost savings.[19] Less than a third of the rules with quantified benefits include monetized benefits. I relate the difference, in part, to specific agency policies stemming from statutory limitations restricting the consideration of benefits or costs. OSHA, for example, is restricted from using a benefit-cost framework as a basis for health standards. While the agency quantifies significant benefits with human impacts in all fifteen rules examined in this study, OSHA monetized those benefits in only one case. I later examine the implications of attaching a dollar value to quantified benefits that the agency did not monetize.

Table 3-2 shows a detailed breakdown for the EPA because the majority of regulations promulgated from 1981 to mid-1996 are EPA regulations. The table shows that the agency assessed costs for nearly all their rules but did not quantify benefits or cost savings for twenty of the rules. Many of the rules lacking benefit estimates are process-oriented, such as rules that require third parties to gather information or outline the structure of

Table 3-1 Regulatory Scorecard, 1981 to Mid-1996

	Total	CPSC	DOL-Health	DOL-Safety	DOT	EPA	HHS	HUD	USDA
Number of rules[a]	168	1	15	13	13	115	5	2	4
Costs assessed	164	1	15	13	13	111	5	2	4
	98%	100%	100%	100%	100%	97%	100%	100%	100%
Benefits or cost savings assessed[b]	146	1	15	13	13	95	5	2	2
	87%	100%	100%	100%	100%	83%	100%	100%	50%
Benefits monetized	44	1	1	3	4	26	5	2	2
	26%	100%	7%	23%	31%	23%	100%	100%	50%

Notes: CPSC = Consumer Product Safety Commission; DOL = Department of Labor; DOT = Department of Transportation; EPA = Environmental Protection Agency; HHS = Department of Health and Human Services; HUD = Department of Housing and Urban Development; and USDA = Department of Agriculture.

a. The scorecard includes 121 final rules and 47 proposed rules.

b. This category includes fatal and nonfatal human health benefits from reduction in the risk of cancer, heart disease, lead poisoning, and car, fire, and workplace accidents. The category also includes benefits from pollution reduction and any other benefits or cost savings that the agency quantified or monetized.

Table 3-2 Regulatory Scorecard: Breakdown for Environmental Statutes, 1981 to Mid-1996

	EPA	CAA	CERCLA	CWA	FIFRA	RCRA	SDWA	TSCA
Number of rules[a]	115	62	5	14	2	19	8	5
Costs assessed	111	61	5	13	2	17	8	5
	97%	98%	100%	93%	100%	89%	100%	100%
Benefits or cost savings assessed[b]	95	55	0	12	1	17	7	3
	83%	89%	0%	86%	50%	89%	88%	60%
Benefits monetized	26	13	0	7	0	2	3	1
	23%	21%	0%	50%	0%	11%	38%	20%

Notes: EPA = Environmental Protection Agency; CAA = Clean Air Act; CERCLA = Comprehensive Environmental Response, Compensation, and Liability Act; CWA = Clean Water Act; FIFRA = Federal Insecticide, Fungicide, and Rodenticide Act; RCRA = Resource Conservation and Recovery Act; SDWA = Safe Drinking Water Act; and TSCA = Toxic Substances Control Act.

a. The scorecard includes eighty-two final rules and thirty-three proposed rules.

b. This category includes fatal and nonfatal human health benefits from reduction in the risk of cancer, heart disease, lead poisoning, and car, fire, and workplace accidents. The category also includes benefits from pollution reduction and any other benefits or cost savings that the agency quantified or monetized.

government programs.[20] The benefits of process-oriented rules are often difficult to identify, much less to quantify.

What Do the U.S. Government's Numbers Tell Us?

As is clear from the previous section, the government's numbers are often the result of incomplete—and sometimes even flawed—analysis. Nevertheless, those numbers are the only available source of data on which we can base a comprehensive review of major regulations. I therefore used those estimates to aggregate the net benefits of regulation and to identify factors that explain variation in regulatory efficiency. But I only report the conclusions that I believe are defensible despite weaknesses in the original data. My assessment of the government's numbers yields four important conclusions. First, aggregate estimates of agency net benefits based on the government's own numbers are positive. Second, the government can increase the net benefits of regulation. Less than half the rules pass a neutral economist's benefit-cost test. Net benefits would increase substantially if agencies rejected such rules. Third, net benefits exhibit a wide range, which suggests that a reallocation of regulatory resources could increase the aggregate net benefits of regulation. Fourth, we can explain some of the variability in regulatory efficiency by using regression analysis. Regulations designed to reduce cancer risks, for example, are less cost-effective than other regulations. More research is necessary, however, to understand fully why significant variation exists. Here, I describe the methodology I used to aggregate and compare the government's estimates of the benefits and costs of regulation, the results of the sensitivity analysis, and the results of a regression analysis designed to explain the observed variation in efficiency among regulations.

Methodology. I used the government's numbers provided in the regulatory impact analyses to aggregate the benefits and costs of regulations from 1981 to mid-1996, to determine which regulations pass a benefit-cost test, and to identify factors that explain variation in the estimates of regulatory cost-effectiveness.[21] My analysis of the RIAs took agency estimates of the impact of regulations on the economy as given. I used those agency estimates to calculate the present value of the benefits and costs of a particular regulation or regulatory alternative. I then calculated the net benefits of each regulation, defined as the difference between benefits and costs, and aggregated the net benefits of all regulations. I also calculated the net benefits of regulation by agency and by environmental statute. I further calculated the cost-effectiveness of regulations by dividing the cost of the regulation by the benefits, such as the number of lives saved.

To make the analysis consistent across different programs and regulations and to allow for aggregation of net benefits, I converted all dollar estimates to the same dollar base year. In that way I corrected for inflation and further discounted all dollar estimates to reflect the social opportunity cost of investing in the regulation. I first used the consumer price index to convert all annualized estimates of costs and benefits for each regulation to 1995 dollars. Next, I aggregated the benefits and costs of each regulation by using the base year of implementation that the agency identified in the RIA. If the agency did not identify a base year, I used the year after the date the agency published the regulation in the *Federal Register* as the base year. Finally, using 1996 as the base year, I calculated the present value of the net benefits of all regulations. If a rule reported costs or benefits from a year after 1996, for example, I discounted values back to 1996. Likewise, if a rule had benefits and costs before 1996, I discounted the values forward to 1996. I describe how varying the base year affects my final estimates later in this section, when I discuss the results of my analysis.

I also introduced a common discount rate because agencies often chose different discount rates for their analyses. The real discount rate for the base case is 5 percent, with 3 percent and 7 percent used in the sensitivity analyses. I discussed the choice of discount rate in more detail in my original study.[22] I also monetized some benefits that the agencies chose not to monetize. For health risk reduction regulations, agencies often provided estimates of the number of lives the agency expected the rule to save, in addition to the number of injuries the agency expected the rule to avert. To monetize those benefits, I used standard willingness-to-pay estimates based on labor market studies of risk-dollar tradeoffs for fatal and nonfatal risks. Willingness-to-pay estimates represent the amount an individual is willing to pay to reduce a specified risk or to protect the environment. The willingness to pay to avoid a risk of fatality is referred to as the implicit "value of life."[23] The value of life for the base case is $5 million, with values of $3 million and $7 million used in the sensitivity analyses.[24] I further used a consistent set of willingness-to-pay values for reducing nonfatal risks of injury and disease, called a fatality index, since those values also varied by agency.[25] I valued a chronic disease or disabling injury at one-third of a life, workday-lost injuries at a hundredth of a life, and non-workday-lost injuries at two-hundredths of a life, on the basis of work by the Department of Transportation's National Highway Traffic Safety Administration and work summarized by Viscusi.[26] I adjusted nonfatal injuries from car accidents by using NHTSA's equivalent life calculation.[27] For the value of reducing a unit of pollution for the five air pollutants in the database, I

Table 3-3 **Key Parameters of the Model**

Parameter	Low Value	Base Value	High Value
Discount rate	3%	5%	7%
Implicit value of life	$3,000,000	$5,000,000	$7,000,000
Value of pollution benefits (per ton)			
Carbon monoxide	$0	$0	$100
Hydrocarbons	$100	$1,000	$2,500
Nitrogen oxides	$100	$1,000	$2,500
Particulate matter (PM 10)	$2,500	$10,000	$30,000
Sulfur dioxide	$100	$700	$1,000

Note: I adjusted all dollar figures to 1994 dollars by using implicit price deflators (Council of Economic Advisers 1995). I updated those figures to 1995 dollars in the rest of this chapter

based my estimates on previously published studies and selected numbers from the EPA's RIAs.[28] All agencies, including the EPA, did not often provide quantified estimates of environmental benefits other than air pollution reduction benefits. My analysis therefore includes only air pollution reduction benefits. To calculate the total benefits of a rule, I combined the benefits from health and safety risk reduction with the benefits from air pollution reduction. The estimates of air pollution reduction benefits may, however, include some benefits from morbidity and mortality risk reduction in addition to environmental protection. Consequently, a possibility of overlap exists between the air pollution reduction estimates and the health and safety risk reduction estimates because both may include benefits from reducing mortality and morbidity. The effect of the overlap is small, however, because it pertains only to the benefits from reducing cancer risk. Of all the pollutants included in the analysis, only the estimates of the benefits of reducing particulate matter and sulfur dioxide appear to include mortality benefits. The mortality benefits do not significantly overlap with the benefits of reducing cancer risk, and I therefore do not believe that the overlap affects the results of my analysis. Table 3-3 summarizes values for key parameters.

Unless otherwise specified, I presumed that regulations would be in force for at least twenty years. If the RIA specified a longer time frame, I used that time frame. If benefits accrued over a longer time frame because a disease or illness had a latency period between the exposure and the onset of the problem, I discounted the benefits back to the present. If the stream of benefits was not given, I discounted the average annual benefits by using average latency periods. If the agency specified a preferred alternative or scenario in the RIA or the *Federal Register* notice, I evaluated that alternative. If the agency did not specify a preferred alternative, I examined an average of the most likely set of alternatives.

Positive Net Benefits of Regulation from 1981 to Mid-1996. The net benefits of federal regulation approach a net present value of $1.8 trillion for final rules and $386 billion for proposed rules.[29] More regulations in the database have negative net benefits than positive net benefits.[30] Rules with positive net benefits average about $45 million in net benefits, however, while rules with negative net benefits average about –$4.5 million. Table 3-4 summarizes the results of the analysis.[31] Table 3-5 analyzes EPA rules in more detail on the basis of specific statutes because about two-thirds of the final rules are EPA rules. Table 3-4 covers thirty-two fewer regulations than table 3-1 because I excluded some rules to represent more accurately the impact of regulations over the time period.[32] The table provides aggregate estimates for each agency as well as a combined estimate for all agencies. The first part of the table summarizes the results for final rules, and the second part summarizes the results for proposed rules.[33] In each section of the table, I list the number of regulations for which either cost or benefit and cost information was available and provide aggregate information on benefits and costs. It is clear from the table that although the total net benefits of regulation are positive, net benefits vary dramatically by agency.

Table 3-4 shows that aggregate net benefits are positive for final rules from each agency with the exception of the Department of Health and Human Services.[34] That is not true for proposed rules, as only the Department of Labor, the EPA, and the Department of Health and Human Services have positive aggregate benefits.[35] The analysis indicates that safety regulations, which reduce the risk of car, fire, or workplace accidents, have higher net benefits than other regulations. DOL safety regulations, for example, have higher net benefits than DOL health regulations for both final and proposed rules. In addition, the net benefits of Department of Transportation regulations, designed primarily to increase motor vehicle safety, far exceed the net benefits of other agencies. The net benefits of DOT regulations account for over half the total net benefits from regulation, although those net benefits result from less than 10 percent of all regulations used to calculate net benefits.

The net benefits of EPA regulations account for approximately one-quarter of the total net benefits of final regulations, yet the EPA promulgated 66 percent of the final regulations in the database. In addition, the EPA's net benefits are positive only because of nineteen Clean Air Act rules with high net benefits. All EPA rules promulgated under the Comprehensive

Table 3-4 Net Benefits of Regulations, 1981 to Mid-1996

	Total	CPSC	DOL-Health	DOL-Safety	DOT	EPA	HHS	HUD	USDA
Final									
Number of regulations	106	1	9	10	9	70	3	1	3
Gross cost	$106.9	$1.3	$43.8	$20.6	$59.9	$444.0	$29.0	$.9	$2.5
Net cost	$395.8	$.7	$43.8	–$15.3	$53.1	$283.6	$28.5	–$.9	$2.5
Benefits	$2,172.2	$7.1	$65.4	$96.1	$1,186.9	$773.8	$23.9	$.1	$18.9
Net benefits[a]	$1,776.4	$6.4	$21.6	$111.5	$1,133.8	$490.3	–$4.6	$1.1	$16.5
Proposed									
Number of regulations	30	—	3	1	3	19	2	1	1
Gross cost	$100.8	—	$2.7	$1.8	$4.0	$84.7	$3.5	$1.3	$2.7
Net cost	$37.3	—	$2.7	$1.8	$3.7	$65.1	–$39.7	$.9	$2.7
Benefits	$423.2	—	$5.5	$46.2	$3.4	$93.6	$274.6	$.0	$.0
Net benefits[a]	$386.0	—	$2.7	$44.4	–$.3	$28.5	$314.3	–$.9	–$2.7

Notes: CPSC = Consumer Product Safety Commission; DOL = Department of Labor; DOT = Department of Transportation; EPA = Environmental Protection Agency; HHS = Department of Health and Human Services; HUD = Department of Housing and Urban Development; and USDA = Department of Agriculture. All figures are in billions of 1995 dollars. The aggregate totals may not add because of rounding.

a. I calculated net benefits by subtracting net costs from benefits.

Table 3-5 Net Benefits of Regulations: Breakdown for Environmental Statutes, 1981 to Mid-1996

	EPA	CAA	CERCLA	CWA	FIFRA	RCRA	SDWA	TSCA
Final								
Number of regulations	70	35	5	8	2	11	5	4
Gross cost	$444.0	$192.0	$34.0	$30.7	$7.6	$121.6	$43.6	$14.6
Net cost	$283.6	$127.7	$34.0	$30.2	$7.6	$26.8	$43.6	$13.6
Benefits	$773.8	$714.6	$.0	$1.3	$.0	$.5	$57.2	$.3
Net benefits[a]	$490.3	$586.9	-$34.0	-$29.0	-$7.6	-$26.3	$13.6	-$13.4
Proposed								
Number of regulations	19	10	—	4	—	2	3	—
Gross cost	$84.7	$34.0	—	$6.0	—	$15.7	$28.9	—
Net cost	$65.1	$18.5	—	$2.1	—	$15.6	$28.9	—
Benefits	$93.6	$48.1	—	$.1	—	$.7	$44.7	—
Net benefits[a]	$19.9	$28.2	—	-$2.0	—	-$14.8	$8.6	—

Notes: EPA = Environmental Protection Agency; CAA = Clean Air Act; CERCLA = Comprehensive Environmental Response, Compensation, and Liability Act; CWA = Clean Water Act; FIFRA = Federal Insecticide, Fungicide, and Rodenticide Act; RCRA = Resource Conservation and Recovery Act; SDWA = Safe Drinking Water Act; and TSCA = Toxic Substance Control Act. All figures are in billions of 1995 dollars. The aggregate totals may not add because of rounding.
a. I calculated net benefits by subtracting net costs from benefits.

Environmental Response, Compensation, and Liability Act, the Clean Water Act, the Toxic Substances Control Act, and the Federal Insecticide, Fungicide, and Rodenticide Act have negative net benefits. Since the Toxic Substances Control Act and the Federal Insecticide, Fungicide, and Rodenticide Act are regarded as "balancing" statutes, meaning that they contain statutory language that requires agencies to balance the benefits and costs of regulations, it is remarkable that all EPA rules authorized by those statutes have negative net benefits. A closer look at the two Federal Insecticide, Fungicide, and Rodenticide Act rules and the four Toxic Substances Control Act rules reveals that the EPA either identified benefits for those regulations and did not quantify the benefits or simply did not identify any benefits.[36] Table 3-5 shows that five of seven statutes have regulations that result in net costs. Only regulations based on the Clean Air Act and the Safe Drinking Water Act yield positive net benefits. In the case of the Safe Drinking Water Act, one regulation addressing lead and copper accounts for over 95 percent of the benefits of all the act's regulations. Without one rule that substantially reduces lead content in gasoline, net benefits for the Clean Air Act drop from about $590 billion to just over $200 billion. Proposed regulations show a similar pattern with a wide range of net benefits for regulations.

Figure 3-1 provides an overview of the distribution of net benefits of final rules over time. The results reveal two interesting patterns also found in my earlier study.[37] First, I find no distinct time trend for benefits and costs. Second, most rules with net benefits tend to range from $10 billion to less than $100 billion. In contrast, most rules with net costs range from $100 million to $10 billion.[38] While less than half of all final rules pass a benefit-cost test, the aggregate net benefits are positive because many of the rules that do pass have substantial benefits. For example, just two rules—the DOT's automatic restraints in cars and the EPA's lead phasedown in gasoline—account for just over 70 percent of the total net benefits of regulation.

I examine the impact of varying key parameters on the benefits and costs of individual regulations because I made a number of critical assumptions to standardize the data. Table 3-6 shows the impact of varying the discount rate and the value of benefits for final rules. A reduction in the value of benefits from the base-case scenario to the "low" scenario reduces net benefits at the 5 percent discount rate from $1,776 billion to $746 billion. An increase in the value of net benefits to the "high" scenario increases net benefits to $3,012 billion. Variations in the discount rate have a less pronounced impact. Decreasing the discount rate from 5 percent to 3 percent increases net benefits to $2,050 billion, while increasing the dis-

Figure 3-1 Net Benefits of Final Major Regulations as a Function of Time, 1981–1997 (*n* = 106)

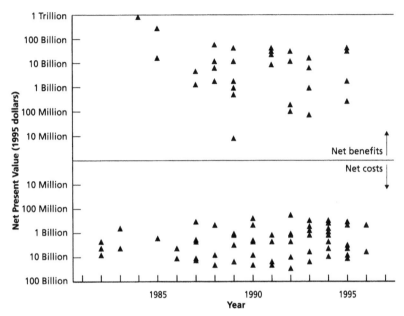

Notes: The figure uses a modified logarithmic scale. The logarithm of net benefits is on the top half of the figure for all rules that have positive net benefits. The logarithm of net costs is on the bottom half of the figure for all rules that have positive net costs.

count rate from 5 percent to 7 percent decreases net benefits to $1,581 billion.[39]

Varying the base year for the present-value calculation significantly affects the magnitude of the estimates. It was necessary to choose a base year to standardize the data, but the choice was difficult because the benefits and costs of regulations accrue over different periods of time from 1981 onward and therefore have different base years. The choice of an earlier base year than 1996, the year that I chose for this analysis, lowers the net benefits of regulations because the value of benefits in the future decreases for regulations promulgated later. If I used a different base year, all net benefits would change by a factor of $(1 + r)^t$, where r is the discount rate and t is the difference between the new and the original base year. For example, with a 5 percent discount rate and 1980 as a base year instead of 1996, the analysis would yield the present value of net benefits at roughly half the original estimate. Similarly, using 2010 as the base year would nearly double the present-value estimate. That analysis suggests that we need to treat the aggregate benefit numbers with great care because no obvious choice for a base year exists. I chose 1996 for the base year because

Table 3-6 Sensitivity Analysis of the Net Benefits of Final Rules

Value of Benefits	Discount Rate		
	3%	5%	7%
Low	$873	$746	$656
Base	$2,050	$1,776	$1,581
High	$3,465	$3,012	$2,688

Note: All estimates are in billions of 1995 dollars.

that was the "present" for my analysis. I could just as easily have chosen 1980 or 1981, however, in which case I would have obtained a substantially lower estimate.

In addition, the choice of a base year greatly affects how net benefits vary with changes in the discount rate. Figure 3-2 shows the net benefits as a function of the discount rate for base years 1980, 1996, and 2010. Table 3-6 shows how total net benefits vary with changes in the discount rate. For the 1980 case, all parts of the benefit-cost stream are discounted backward because all rules are implemented after 1980. In addition, as figure 3-1 shows, the aggregate net present value of benefits from regulations implemented in any given year is positive for most years.[40] Therefore, I observe a decline in net present value as the discount rate increases.[41] In contrast, for the 2010 case, most parts of the benefit-cost stream would be discounted forward, so I observe an increase in net benefits as the discount rate increases. For 1996, the base year used in the calculations of this chapter, some parts of the benefit-cost stream are discounted forward, while others are discounted backward. The net effect is that net benefits decrease as the discount rate increases. Varying values for other parameters, such as the average age at death, latency periods, and derivation of the fatality index, generally has a less pronounced effect on the results.

The Relative Efficiency of Regulations. A regulation's benefit-cost ratio or its estimated cost-effectiveness is a measure of its efficiency. If society spends its regulatory resources efficiently, it maximizes the net benefits of regulation. While cost-effectiveness estimates and benefit-cost ratios are not better measures of efficiency than estimates of net benefits, they allow us to compare regulations if the information about regulatory benefits and costs is insufficient to estimate net benefits. In environmental, health, and safety regulation, a common definition of cost-effectiveness is the resources used for each statistical life saved by the regulation.[42] A benefit-cost ratio is the sum of the benefits and cost savings from a regulation divided by the costs of the regulation. Here, I use cost-effectiveness estimates and benefit-cost ratios primarily to examine factors that could explain the variation in regulatory efficiency.

Figure 3-2 Aggregate Net Benefits of Final Regulations as a Function of the Discount Rate (base-case benefit values)

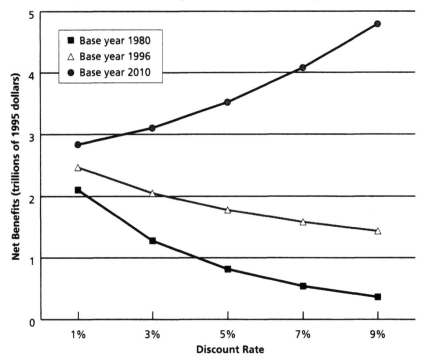

The regression analysis based on cost-effectiveness estimates produces four results. First, regulations that address cancer risks are generally less cost-effective than other regulations. Second, cancer regulations promulgated by the EPA appear less cost-effective than other cancer regulations. Third, measuring whether the Office of Information and Regulatory Affairs has increased the efficiency of the regulatory process is difficult.[43] Finally, the cost-effectiveness of regulations does not vary systematically over time.[44] Figure 3-3 graphs the logarithm of the cost-effectiveness of each regulation, identified by the year of promulgation, against time.[45] Figure 3-3 shows that the cost-effectiveness of regulation exhibits a wide variation over time, within agencies and across agencies. Cost-effectiveness estimates range from $60,000 to $38 billion per life saved, with a median value of about $6 million per life saved. To put the cost-effectiveness estimates in perspective, if the government spent the entire gross national product on reducing accidental deaths and environmentally induced cancers, the maximum the government could spend per life saved is $68 million.[46] If I applied that "GNP test" to all final regulations, 25 percent—thirteen of fifty-two—would fail. For the EPA, 50 percent—twelve of twenty-four—would fail the test.[47]

Figure 3-3 Cost-Effectiveness of Selected Final Environmental, Health, and Safety Regulations (*n* = 52)

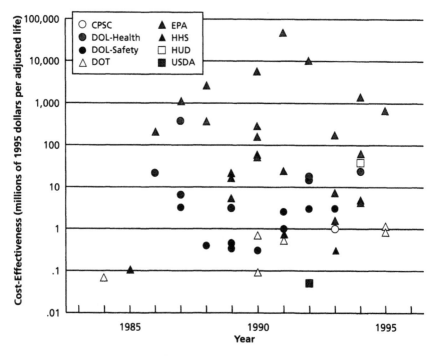

Note: CPSC = Consumer Product Safety Commission: DOL = Department of Labor; DOT = Department of Transportation; EPA = Environmental Protection Agency; HHS = Department of Health and Human Services; HUD = Department of Housing and Urban Development; and USDA = Department of Agriculture.

In other words, for a significant number of regulations, the government would exhaust the GNP simply by investing in regulations aimed at reducing a small portion of the cancer risk that society faces. Such imprudent investments leave no money for the basic necessities of life. The high cost-effectiveness estimates and the variability in cost-effectiveness across regulations and agencies suggest that we can achieve much greater risk reduction at a lower cost to society, a point several authors have made.[48]

Table 3-7 summarizes three cost-effectiveness regressions and one benefit-cost ratio regression.[49] One of the cost-effectiveness regressions is based on the data assembled for this study, and the other two combine data from the study with data from earlier studies by Morrall.[50] The dependent variable in all regressions is the natural logarithm of the cost-effectiveness of regulation.[51] For the Hahn regression I used the natural logarithm of the cost per life-year saved, and for the Hahn-Morrall pooled regression I used

Table 3-7 Regression Results

Cost-Effectiveness[a]	n	R^2	Constant	Year	Cancer	EPA-Cancer	OIRA
Hahn	52	.662	–181.72	.089 (.9)	3.62* (4.1)	2.17* (2.5)	
Hahn-Morrall	81	.643	–91.1	.05 (1.3)	3.76* (6.2)	1.06* (1.7)	
Hahn-Morrall/OIRA	81	.652	–215.6	.11* (1.9)	3.67* (6.1)	1.21* (1.9)	1.38 (1.4)
Benefit-Cost Ratio[b]	**n**	**R^2**	**Constant**	**Year**	**Health**	**EPA-Health**	
Hahn	105	.187	–270.6	.14 (1.4)	–3.21* (–2.7)	–.45* (–.5)	

Notes: All regressions use only final rules. All variables with a t-statistic that is significant at the 10 percent level using a tow-tailed test are marked with an asterisk. The t-statistics appear in parentheses.

a. The dependent variable in the Hahn cost-effectiveness regression is the natural logarithm of the cost per adjusted life-year saved. The dependent variable in the Hahn and Morrall pooled cost-effectiveness regression is the cost per life saved. 1 adjusted life-years and lives on the basis of a fatality index that Viscusi (1992) created. See the description in the text for more information.

b. The dependent variable in the Hahn benefit-cost ratio regression is the natural logarithm of the adjusted benefit-cost ratio. The benefit-cost ratio is defined as the sum of benefits and cost savings divided by gross costs. The benefits include life-years saved, which are adjusted on the basis of a fatality index that Viscusi (1992) created. See the description in the text for more information. I adjusted the logarithm by a small constant to include zero values.

the natural logarithm of the cost per life saved.[52] I also used slightly different estimates for the cancer variable in the Hahn regression. The Hahn-Morrall/OIRA regression adds to the Hahn-Morrall pooled regression a dummy variable for regulations promulgated before the creation of OIRA. I used only final regulations for all regressions.[53] I tested four hypotheses: (1) cancer regulations are less cost-effective than other regulations; (2) cancer regulations promulgated by the EPA are less cost-effective than other cancer regulations; (3) regulations promulgated before the creation of OIRA are less cost-effective than other regulations;[54] and (4) regulations have decreased in cost-effectiveness over time, as measured by the date the agency published the rule in the *Federal Register*.[55]

I expected that a regulation designed to reduce the risk of cancer would be less cost-effective than other regulations because agencies appear to regulate cancer risks more stringently than noncancer risks. Agencies may, for example, regulate cancer risks more stringently because of public dread of cancer risks, a factor that may translate into political support for cancer regulations.[56] Figure 3-4, which is based on the same data on final environmental, health, and safety regulations used for figure 3-3, illustrates that regulations designed to reduce cancer risk are generally less cost-effective than regulations that are not designed to reduce cancer risk. The median cancer regulation, for example, is over seventy times as costly per life saved as the median noncancer regulation.[57] On the basis of a review of the data and research of other economists, I also expected that cancer regulations promulgated by the EPA are less cost-effective than other cancer regulations. Figure 3-3, for example, suggests that EPA regulations in general are relatively poor in terms of cost-effectiveness compared with the regulations of other agencies. The median final EPA regulation costs about $120 million per life saved, more than eight times higher than the median for DOL health regulations and more than eighty times higher than the median for all other agencies.[58] It is not clear from figure 3-3, however, whether EPA regulations are less cost-effective because they are EPA regulations or because they are cancer regulations.[59]

I further expected that regulations promulgated before the creation of OIRA are less cost-effective than regulations promulgated after the creation of OIRA because of the positive impact of OIRA review of draft regulations. I only tested that variable in the Hahn-Morrall pooled regression because my original data set does not contain any regulations before the creation of OIRA. Finally, I presumed that cost-effectiveness declines over time as agencies use the low-cost options for saving lives first, although new scientific information about risk or the introduction of new technologies to reduce risk could reverse that effect.

Figure 3-4 Cost-Effectiveness of Selected Environmental, Health, and Safety Regulations (*n* = 52)

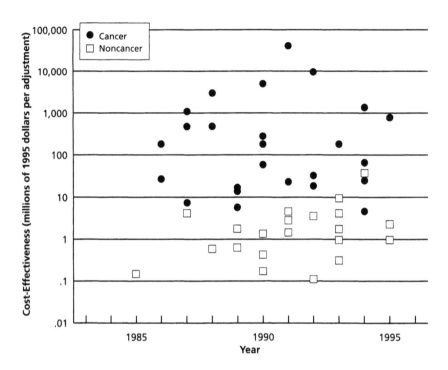

The results of the Hahn regression and the two regressions based on the Hahn-Morrall pooled data are similar. Cancer is the only variable that is highly significant in all three regressions.[60] The magnitude of the difference in cost-effectiveness between cancer regulations and other social regulations is somewhat surprising. My analysis suggests that cancer regulations are approximately forty-two times less cost-effective than other regulations. Cancer regulations could be as little as 5 times less cost-effective or as great as 142 times less cost-effective than other social regulations.[61] The existing evidence that EPA cancer regulations are less cost-effective than other cancer regulations is not convincing because the coefficient is only marginally significant.[62] The results from the Hahn-Morrall pooled regression show that cancer regulations are approximately twice as cost-effective as EPA cancer regulations, although the EPA cancer regulations could be slightly more cost-effective than other cancer regulations or as much as nine times less cost-effective.[63] More research is necessary to determine whether EPA cancer regulations are more or less cost-effective than other cancer regulations.[64]

Contrary to my expectations, the OIRA variable is not significant.[65] The lack of evidence of OIRA's impact on the process appears to result from a lack of observations before the creation of OIRA and the difficulty of finding an appropriate measure of OIRA's impact. Why OIRA review does not significantly affect cost-effectiveness estimates is unclear, although that result is probably a function of the lack of adequate data before the creation of OIRA.[66] Only ten rules in the Hahn-Morrall data set were promulgated before the creation of OIRA. Alternatively, the data may mask the impact of OIRA because agencies simply did not propose or finalize rules for several years after the creation of OIRA. For example, the Hahn-Morrall pooled data set for 1981 and 1982—the first two years after the creation of OIRA—had no cost-effectiveness estimates for regulations. Another possibility is that measuring the impact of OIRA from information on the benefits and costs of final rules is difficult. The impact of OIRA may, for example, be integrally tied to high-level political officials' delaying, modifying, and rejecting rules. We cannot easily observe such actions. Measuring how suggestions OIRA made to the agencies might have changed the cost-effectiveness of a regulation is also difficult. Further analysis is therefore necessary to determine the extent to which OIRA has affected the cost-effectiveness of regulations.[67]

The evidence that the year of promulgation does not influence cost-effectiveness is strong, and the result is consistent with figure 3-3. Figure 3-3 shows that the cost-effectiveness of regulations as a function of time does not follow any obvious pattern.[68] The result could arise for several reasons. For example, new hazards that may result in relatively cost-effective regulation continuously emerge. In addition, differences in the priorities of different administrations could affect cost-effectiveness estimates.[69] Another possible explanation is simply that concerns with cost-effectiveness rarely drive agencies' agendas. Instead, they are driven by laws that Congress passes as crises arise from time to time. I have found some evidence that agencies do not set priorities on the basis of relative risks or cost-effectiveness. The EPA, for example, only recently began seriously examining the relative rankings of risks.[70] Even to this day, the agency has done very little work on prioritizing regulations in terms of cost-effectiveness. The same is true of most other agencies. Another possible explanation is that social regulation had reached the point of diminishing returns by the early 1980s. Congress passed most of the major environmental statutes, such as the most comprehensive versions of the Clean Water Act and the Clear Air Act, in the early 1970s. A time series dating back to the early 1970s might therefore show a time trend. Finally, technological improvement may lower the cost of meeting some regulatory objectives.

The benefit-cost ratio regression, which includes regulations with no quantified benefits and regulations with air pollution reduction benefits that are not included in the cost-effectiveness estimates, provides an alternative measure of regulatory efficiency.[71] The results of the benefit-cost ratio regression, presented in table 3-7, support the results of the cost-effectiveness regressions. Health regulations, which reduce the risk of cancer, heart disease, and lead poisoning, have lower benefit-cost ratios than safety regulations, which reduce the risk of car, fire, or work-related accidents. In addition, EPA health regulations appear to have lower benefit-cost ratios than other health regulations. Finally, the benefit-cost ratios of regulations do not vary systematically over time.

A benefit-cost ratio is the sum of benefits and cost savings divided by gross costs.[72] The benefit-cost ratio database contains 105 regulations, 24 more than the cost-effectiveness regression.[73] The regression is based only on data collected for this study and does not include regulations from the Morrall database used for the cost-effectiveness regressions. The benefit-cost ratio regression uses the natural logarithm of the benefit-cost ratio as the dependent variable[74] and a health variable instead of the cancer variable used in the cost-effectiveness regressions.[75] Of the 105 regulations in the database, 84 are health regulations. The regulations span from 1982 to 1996, but 67 percent of the regulations are from 1990 to 1996. The database has twenty-five regulations with zero benefits because the agency did not quantify benefits or cost savings but did include some estimate of the costs of the regulation.[76] While most of the benefit-cost ratios for regulations are low (55 percent of regulations have a ratio that is less than one), eight benefit-cost ratios in the database range from twelve to sixty-one. Of the eight regulations, five are safety regulations and three are health regulations.

Similar to the cost-effectiveness regressions, the benefit-cost ratio regression was designed to test the hypotheses that health regulations are less efficient than other social regulations, that EPA health regulations are less efficient than other health regulations, and that the benefit-cost ratios of regulations have decreased over time. The results of the benefit-cost ratio regression are similar to the cost-effectiveness regressions because the health variable is significant and the EPA variable and the year variable are both insignificant. The signs on both the EPA and the health variables are negative, as expected. The analysis strongly suggests that health regulations have lower benefit-cost ratios than other regulations, but it provides less support for the hypothesis that EPA health regulations have lower benefit-cost ratios than other regulations because of complications from collinearity.[77]

The limitations of the original data may affect the results of the regressions. Although this analysis is more comprehensive than any other analysis to date, I based the regressions on only a subset of my original database because of the absence of benefit and cost estimates for the majority of the regulations. In addition, technological advances and scientific discoveries may reveal that agencies originally understated the benefits of existing rules. Finally, variation in the assumptions agencies and program offices use to estimate benefits and costs affects the results of such analytical exercises. I have therefore primarily designed the regressions to provide an initial starting point from which to launch a more thorough investigation of the factors that influence the efficiency of regulations.

Statutory Restrictions on Regulations and Economic Efficiency

Information on the political forces that affect regulations may explain some variability in regulatory efficiency. Political forces affect the efficiency of regulations because each statute is the product of a legislative debate that reflects the beliefs of individual representatives as well as the prevailing degree of public support for regulatory reform. The often heated and partisan discourse creates a significant amount of variation in the stringency of statutory requirements that should determine the degree to which agencies balance the benefits and costs of regulations. To ascertain whether balancing requirements affect regulatory outcomes, I first examined the degree to which statutes allow agencies to consider benefits and costs in the process of designing regulations.[78] I then compared the net benefits of regulations promulgated under the different statutes. I find that statutory limitations appear to have little effect on the efficiency of rules.

The statutory language that requires agencies to consider benefits and costs varies tremendously across and even within statutes, and the language is often ambiguous.[79] Agencies and courts have determined that some statutes preclude agencies from considering costs. Numerous environmental, health, and safety statutes, such as the Occupational Safety and Health Act and most parts of the Clean Air Act, restrict the use of benefit-cost analysis in regulatory decisionmaking. Congress attempted to address widespread concern about statutory restrictions on balancing benefits and costs with a "supermandate" provision in some of the more recently proposed regulatory reform bills. A supermandate provision means that the balancing language in the regulatory reform bill will supplement and—to the extent conflict exists—supersede requirements of authorizing statutes. One bill required agencies to apply a limited benefit-cost test to proposed and final regulations.[80] To examine the possible effect of restrictions on the expected benefits from regulations, I place statutes into two categories—statutes that allow balancing and statutes that bar or restrict balancing.[81] While the categorization is crude, the methodology allows a rough comparison of rules resulting from the two types of statutes. The balancing language in two statutes, the Resource Conservation and Recovery Act and safety standards under the Occupational Safety and Health Act, does not specify whether the agencies should consider benefits and costs during the rulemaking process. The agencies have, however, often interpreted the statutes to limit the consideration of costs.[82] Hence, I consider two scenarios—one that designates the two statutes as a separate category and one that includes the two statutes in the balancing barred or restricted category. I then use the information from the regulatory scorecard and the net benefits of regulations to sort the regulations into the categories shown in table 3-8. I hypothesize that rules from limiting statutes are less economically efficient than rules resulting from other statutes. Hence, a lower percentage of those rules would pass a benefit-cost test.[83]

The analysis leads to the following conclusions. First, the degree to which agencies can consider benefits and costs varies tremendously and is often dependent on agency interpretation. Second, most rules are authorized under statutes that allow limited balancing.[84] Many of those rules are EPA rules. Third, while the type of analysis conducted across and within agencies varies tremendously, rules from statutes without limitations on balancing pass a benefit-cost test according to agency analyses more frequently than do rules from statutes with limitations (48 percent versus 15 percent).[85] Such a pattern does not hold within the EPA.[86] Fourth, a clear pattern does not emerge when I examine the frequency that rules pass a benefit-cost test according to my calculations (50 percent versus 38 percent).[87] The analysis of the frequency of rules that pass a benefit-cost test in different categories is quite sensitive to the valuation of health and welfare benefits. The percentage of Clean Air Act rules that pass a benefit-cost test, for example, drops from 54 percent to 20 percent when I use the low valuation of pollution benefits.

Although this preliminary analysis suggests that statutory limitations appear to have little effect on the efficiency of rules, we must interpret the results with care. My analysis uses very crude measures for the degree to which statutes constrain agencies. Moreover, isolating the impact of any single factor in the complex regulatory process is difficult, as the statistical analysis in the previous section shows. Finally, my analysis does not attempt to measure the efficiency gains associated with alternatives the agencies did not select or consider as a result of the restrictions.[88]

Table 3-8 Statutory Treatment of Balancing

	Agency Analyses[a]		Author's Calculations[b]	
	Number of Rules	Benefits Exceed Costs	Number of Rules	Benefits Exceed Costs
Balancing allowed[c]	15	20%	15	47%
Balancing barred/restricted[d]	71	14%	63	37%
Unclear[e]	25	32%	19	53%
Subtotal of balancing barred/restricted and unclear[f]	96	19%	82	40%

a. These numbers are based on an analysis of all final rules from 1981 through mid-1996. The rules are the same final ones used in tables 3-1 and 3-2.
b. These numbers are based on an analysis of final rules from 1981 through mid-1996. The rules are the same ones used to calculate aggregate net benefits. The results of the net benefits analysis are separated by agency in tables 3-4 and 3-5.
c. Statutes include the Oil Pollution Act (DOT), the Transportation Safety Act (DOT), the Federal Insecticide, Fungicide, and Rodenticide Act (EPA), the Toxic Substances Control Act (EPA), and the Food, Drug, and Cosmetic Act (HHS). Note that FIFRA does not limit the balancing of benefits and costs in general rulemaking. The statute does, however, place such limits in setting registration requirements. I therefore place the FIFRA rules that apply to registration requirements in the balancing barred/restricted category.
d. Statutes include the Occupational Safety and Health Act (DOL-Health), the Comprehensive Environmental Response, Compensation, and Liability Act (EPA), the Clean Water Act (EPA), the Federal Insecticide, Fungicide, and Rodenticide Act (EPA), and the Safe Drinking Water Act (EPA).
e. Statutes include the Occupational Safety and Health Act (DOL-Safety) and the Resource Conservation and Recovery Act (EPA).
f. The subtotal represents all statutes that could arguably be placed in the balancing barred/restricted category.

The Influence of Regulatory Impact Analyses on the Regulatory Process

Scholars have undertaken less work to determine the impact of RIAs on the regulatory process than to identify analytical flaws in analyses. Since the impact of RIAs is difficult to measure, the literature has only provided anecdotal evidence of impacts on the process. In a few cases, for example, RIAs have had a substantial impact and have led to more efficient rulemaking.[89] In other cases, RIAs did not aid the rulemaking process, or agencies just used the RIAs to help justify political decisions. Furthermore, agencies often could not use the RIAs because some statutes preclude the balancing of benefits and costs or the consideration of costs. To address the gap in the academic literature, I applied a benefit-cost test to the regulations in my database. The purpose of the test is to determine whether agencies appear to use information on the relationship between benefits and costs to make regulatory decisions. I expected that a high percentage of the regulations would pass a benefit-cost test if agencies consistently use the RIA information to make decisions. I found, however, that the majority of regulations do not pass a benefit-cost test. I also surveyed agency officials to get a sense of the internal view of the impact of economic analysis on the regulatory process. My preliminary research suggests that economic analysis does not have a significant impact on the regulatory process, although more research is necessary to evaluate the impact fully.

For the purpose of this analysis, a rule passes a benefit-cost test if the quantified monetary benefits exceed quantified costs. Table 3-9 shows the fraction of regulations that agencies stated would pass a benefit-cost test and that I found would pass a benefit-cost test after I standardized the agency's numbers.[90] I found that agencies stated that a rule passes a benefit-cost test for 23 percent of all rules—39 of 168. Agencies did not monetize benefits for many of those rules, however. Nine rules pass a benefit-cost test without monetizing benefits because of net cost savings. Of the rules for which the agency monetized benefits, 75 percent—thirty of forty-four—pass a benefit-cost test.[91] Of the twenty-six EPA rules that monetize benefits, fifteen pass the benefit-cost test. An additional four rules pass the test without monetizing benefits because of significant cost savings.

Since agencies often did not monetize benefits and used different assumptions to estimate benefits, I standardized the agency estimates and applied the benefit-cost test again. Table 3-9 shows that 43 percent of all rules—46 of 106—pass a benefit-cost test after I standardized the agency numbers. The table also shows that three of thirty-five final EPA regulations would pass a benefit-cost test for statutes other than the Clean Air

Table 3-9 Rules Passing a Benefit-Cost Test

	Total	CPSC	DOL-Health	DOL-Safety	DOT	EPA	HHS	HUD	USDA
All rules[a]	168	1	15	13	13	115	5	2	4
Agency found benefits exceed costs	23%	100%	7%	38%	31%	17%	100%	100%	50%
Final rules[b]	106	1	9	10	9	70	3	1	3
Monetized benefits exceed costs	43%	100%	33%	100%	78%	31%	33%	100%	33%
Proposed rules[b]	30	—	3	1	3	19	2	1	1
Monetized benefits exceed costs	43%	—	33%	100%	33%	42%	100%	0%	0%

	Total	CAA	CERCLA	CWA	FIFRA	RCRA	SDWA	TSCA
All EPA rules[c]	115	62	5	14	2	19	8	5
Agency found benefits exceed costs	17%	16%	0%	21%	0%	16%	25%	20%
Final EPA rules[d]	70	35	5	8	2	11	5	4
Monetized benefits exceed costs	31%	54%	0%	0%	0%	18%	20%	0%
Proposed EPA rules[d]	19	10	—	4	—	2	3	—
Monetized benefits exceed costs	42%	60%	—	25%	—	0%	33%	—

Notes: CPSC = Consumer Product Safety Commission; DOL = Department of Labor; DOT = Department of Transportation; EPA = Environmental Protection Agency; HHS = Department of Health and Human Services; HUD = Department of Housing and Urban Development; USDA = Department of Agriculture; CAA = Clean Air Act; CERCLA = Comprehensive Environmental Response, Compensation, and Liability Act; CWA = Clean Water Act; FIFRA = Federal Insecticide, Fungicide, and Rodenticide Act; RCRA = Resource Conservation and Recovery Act; SDWA = Safe Drinking Water Act; and TSCA = Toxic Substances Control Act.

a. I based this calculation on the universe of rules introduced in table 3-1. The calculation includes 121 final rules and 47 proposed rules. The number of rules presented in the table is the total number of rules in the database. The percentage estimate is the percentage of total rules for which the agencies stated that the benefits exceed the costs.

b. I based the calculations for final rules and proposed rules on the universe of rules introduced in table 3-4. Therefore, I based the calculations on my standardization of the agencies' numbers. The calculations include sixteen fewer final rules and seventeen fewer proposed rules than I included in the calculation for all rules because I excluded some regulations. See note 32 in the text for a description of the excluded rules.

c. I based the calculations for all EPA rules on the universe of rules introduced in table 3-2. The calculations include eighty-two final rules and thirty-three proposed rules.

d. I based the calculations for final and proposed EPA rules on the universe of rules introduced in table 3-5. The calculations include twelve fewer final rules and fourteen fewer proposed rules than I included for all EPA rules because I excluded some rules. See note 32 in the text for a description of the excluded rules.

Table 3-10 **Number of Rules Passing a Benefit-Cost Test**

| | Discount Rate | | |
Value of Benefits	3%	5%	7%
Low	31	31	31
Base	45	46	45
High	50	50	49

Note: The table shows the number of rules passing a benefit-cost test under various assumptions about the discount rate and the value of benefits. A rule passes a benefit-cost test if the benefits of the rule exceed the costs. The analysis is based on standardized agency estimates of net benefits.

Act. Nineteen of thirty-five final regulations would pass for the Clean Air Act. In addition, 43 percent of proposed rules—thirteen of thirty—also pass the test. Absent my adjustment to the agency's numbers, 25 percent of proposed rules—12 of 47—and 22 percent of final rules—27 of 121— pass a benefit-cost test. The higher number of rules that pass with my standardized estimates results largely because I monetize benefits in several cases for which the agencies did not monetize benefits. While all regulations addressing safety risks pass a benefit-cost test, regulations addressing health and environmental risks pass less frequently. In the case of OSHA, for example, only three of nine final health regulations would pass a benefit-cost test. In the case of the EPA, only twenty-two of seventy would pass such a test.

Table 3-10 shows how the number of rules passing a benefit-cost test varies with assumptions about the discount rate and the valuation of benefits. The number of rules that pass a benefit-cost test is most dependent on the value of the benefits. When I use low values at a 5 percent discount rate, fifteen fewer final rules pass a benefit-cost test than in the base case. The values of air pollution reduction predominantly drive that result, as twelve fewer Clean Air Act rules pass the test.[92] When I use high values at a 5 percent discount rate, four additional rules from the Clean Air Act pass a benefit-cost test. In other words, changes in the value of a unit of air pollution reduction have a marked effect on the net benefits of Clean Air Act rules. The analysis also reveals that the number of rules passing a benefit-cost test does not change dramatically when I vary the discount rate for a given value of benefits.

Varying values for other parameters, such as average age of death, latency periods, and derivation of the fatality index, generally does not have a pronounced effect on the number of rules that pass a benefit-cost test. The number of rules that pass a benefit-cost test does not change when I value lives instead of life-years, for example. Similarly, while over 65 percent of the benefits from NHTSA are nonfatal, all the final rules still have positive net benefits, even when I quantify only benefits from reduced fatalities. That sensitivity analysis suggests that my estimates of the number of rules that pass a benefit-cost test are relatively robust.[93]

The reader should consider factors other than varying key parameters when interpreting my results. To calculate net benefits, I treat a regulation as a single unit of analysis. Such treatment does not show parts of a regulation that fail a benefit-cost test or that could be improved, even when the impact of the entire rule is positive. Thus, simply because a regulation has positive net benefits does not mean that the agency has maximized net benefits or that the agency could not have improved the regulation. The EPA, for example, could have achieved significantly higher net benefits had it refined its rule to reduce exposure to copper and lead in drinking water. Similarly, OSHA could have refined its rule to limit asbestos to achieve very similar results at a much lower cost.[94]

My analysis thus far implies that agencies do not seriously consider the relationship between benefits and costs when making regulatory decisions. I cannot fully support such a conclusion because of the degree of uncertainty associated with the estimates of the benefits and costs of regulation that I outlined in the preceding section. Also, measuring the impact of the RIA is difficult because doing so requires extensive interviews with agency officials. I performed some sensitivity analysis of my final tallies because of that uncertainty. The analysis of the information provided in RIAs provides only summary information about the use of economic analysis in the rulemaking process and excludes independent agencies because neither Reagan's Executive Order 12291 nor Clinton's Executive Order 12866 covers them.

To obtain more specific information about the impact of economic analysis in executive branch and independent agencies, I interviewed current and past agency officials and examined agency dockets, annual reports, and individual rules and decisions. I focused on the procedures that federal agencies employ to catalog information on the benefits and costs of future and existing regulatory activities.[95] My analysis complements a survey conducted by Thomas J. Bliley, Jr., chairman of the House Committee on Commerce.[96] In 1996 Congressman Bliley sent a survey to federal agencies under the committee's jurisdiction.[97] The survey asked the agencies to explain how they accounted for costs in the regulatory process and requested a list of documents describing that information for fiscal year 1995 and earlier years.

Table 3-11 summarizes the results from the agencies surveyed by Bliley and by Hahn. The table has two parts; the first covers executive agencies, and the second covers independent agencies. For executive agencies the table reports the extent to which they estimate the benefits and costs of new major rules and nonmajor rules and activities. In addition, the table reports whether the agency has attempted to provide aggregate estimates of the economic impacts of its regulations. The second part of the table is the same as the first except that it does not distinguish between major and nonmajor rules, since independent agencies are not subject to oversight under the executive orders. For the most part, I found that the agencies at least superficially comply with requirements for economic analysis. All eight of the executive branch agencies I analyzed prepare RIAs for major rules. In addition, some of those agencies, including OSHA, the EPA, and many operating agencies within the DOT, estimate the benefits and costs of a subset of nonmajor rules and activities. Of the independent agencies, only the Consumer Product Safety Commission and the Nuclear Regulatory Commission generally estimate the benefits and costs of rules and licensing activities.[98] Only a limited number of agencies systematically evaluate the benefits and costs of existing regulatory activities, however. None of the independent agencies provides such cumulative estimates.[99] Of all the executive branch agencies, only the National Highway Traffic Safety Administration and the EPA provide that information. Those two agencies offer only partial estimates, however. NHTSA and the Federal Highway Administration have routinely estimated the cumulative impacts of their programs over time.[100] The EPA has estimated the historical cost of all environmental regulation as well as the benefits and costs of particular programs.[101] Table 3-11 reveals that agencies provide very limited information on the benefits and costs of individual regulations. Moreover, only two agencies attempt to provide aggregate estimates of the impacts of their regulatory programs.[102]

Although agencies rarely provide estimates of aggregate benefits and costs, many review existing programs under statutory requirements, agency initiatives, legislation, and executive programs. Agencies have previously provided measures of success, such as the reduction in the number of pages in the *Code of Federal Regulations,* but have generally not thoroughly assessed the effectiveness of such review efforts. In probably the most rigorous review program among all agencies, NHTSA continually reviews the effectiveness of its existing regulations and often examines whether it has realized the projected benefits and costs.[103] Without comprehensively examining the real savings that have resulted from agency reviews of their existing regulatory structure—a task that is beyond the scope of this study—it is almost impossible to quantify those savings.[104] Thus, I remain skeptical of the benefits that agencies

Table 3-11 Federal Regulatory Agencies' Efforts to Catalog Benefit and Cost Information

Agency	Estimates of the Future Benefits and Costs of New Regulatory Activities		Aggregate Estimates of the Benefits and Costs of Regulatory Activities[a]
	Major Rules[b]	Nonmajor Actions[c]	
Executive			
Department of Agriculture	Partial	No evidence	No
Department of Commerce[d]	Partial	No evidence	No
Department of Energy[d]	Partial	No evidence	No
Department of Housing and Urban Development	Partial	No evidence	No
Environmental Protection Agency	Partial	Partial	Partial
Food and Drug Administration	Partial	Partial	No
National Highway Traffic Safety Administration	Partial	Partial	Partial
Occupational Safety and Health Administration	Partial	Partial	No
Independent			
Commodity Futures Trading Commission	No		No
Consumer Product Safety Commission	Partial		No
Federal Communications Commission	No		No
Federal Deposit Insurance Corporation	Partial		No
Federal Energy Regulatory Commission	No		No
Federal Reserve Board	No		No
Federal Trade Commission	No		No
Nuclear Regulatory Commission	Partial		No
Securities and Exchange Commission	No		No
Surface Transportation Board[d,e]	No		No

a. This category does not imply that an agency does not have enough information to estimate aggregate benefits and costs, but rather that an agency does not provide such information. For example, executive agencies may be able to put together a rough calculation of aggregate benefits and costs by compiling regulatory impact analysis estimates.

b. All executive branch agencies are required to prepare regulatory impact analyses for major or economically significant rules. The analyses do not, however, always include comprehensive or complete estimates of benefits and costs. Hence, I characterize them as "partial."

c. Some agencies frequently estimate the benefits and costs of nonmajor actions. Unfortunately, my examination of the nonmajor universe is not exhaustive. Thus, I am not able to describe the size of the subset of nonmajor rules for which agencies have estimated benefits and costs. For other agencies, I have found no evidence that estimates are provided for nonmajor actions.

d. I have relied primarly on Bliley (1997) for this agency.

e. The Surface Transportation Board replaced the Interstate Commerce Commission in 1996.

claim to have produced from those programs.

Conclusions and Policy Recommendations

My analysis of the impact of federal regulatory activities on the economy shows that the net benefits of regulation are positive, that less than half of final regulations pass a strict benefit-cost test, that the quality of agency regulatory impact analyses is poor, and that the efficiency of regulations varies depending on the agency and the type of risk the regulation is designed to reduce. In sum, society could spend its regulatory dollars more wisely, and a system to allocate regulatory dollars efficiently does not exist. To improve the regulatory process, Congress and the White House must enforce the economic analysis requirements they publicly support. They must take advantage of existing reform proposals—designed on the basis of decades of work by regulatory scholars—to improve agency decisionmaking.[105] The success of such efforts requires high-level political support, adherence to established principles of benefit-cost analysis, and rigorous review of agency analyses of regulations by an independent entity.[106]

This study, along with the work of other scholars, suggests that agencies must improve the quality of regulatory impact analyses. Agencies could dramatically improve the quality of RIAs by standardizing assumptions across analyses, providing a better treatment of uncertainties, defining baselines clearly, using peer-reviewed scholarship when available, and presenting results clearly.[107] In addition, agencies could use retrospective studies of actual impacts to complement prospective studies. Such analyses would provide a better assessment of actual benefits and costs than agencies currently provide and would help agencies improve prospective analytical techniques. The improvement of regulatory impact analyses is important, but it is only one component of a larger reform effort. An effective reform effort requires lawmakers to establish principles for reform and then to identify a feasible reform agenda. Elsewhere, I have articulated those principles in more detail with my colleagues, and we have offered a consensus agenda for reform.[108] Here, I summarize two key points.

First, regulatory reform should increase the accountability of elected officials for the regulations they support. Regulations frequently impose costs on society—sometimes as much as billions of dollars annually—that are higher than many direct government expenditure programs. To a large extent, federal bureaucrats now make many regulatory decisions with the tacit acquiescence of legislators, the president, or both. One way society can hold elected officials accountable is if information on the benefits and costs of regulations is accessible on the Internet. Agencies could, for example, make all regulatory impact analyses available on-line. The government should also provide more information on the benefits and costs of regulation. An annual regulatory accounting statement produced by the OMB or the Council of Economic Advisers or both is a step in the right direction.[109] Such a statement should initially focus on the incremental benefits and costs of regulations, but the OMB or CEA could also develop estimates of the aggregate impacts of regulation where feasible. Congress should require both executive branch agencies and independent regulatory agencies to help produce such estimates. If agencies examine carefully the economic impacts of their regulations on real people more carefully, they will develop more effective and less wasteful regulation.

Second, regulatory reform should place greater emphasis on protecting the economic well-being of consumers and producers. As this analysis has shown, the economic benefits and costs of a regulation are often not a decisive factor in determining whether to implement a rule. It is critical for policymakers to consider significant economic impacts when designing a regulation. Congress must revisit the original statutes and limit the scope of federal regulation to activities that agencies can justify on economic grounds. Congress should also consider establishing a congressional or independent agency responsible for replicating key findings used to support regulations before agencies finalize the regulations.

In a sense, my recipe for reform is deceptively simple. Some would say it is simplistic. It calls for better information to make legislators more accountable and a larger role for economic analysis in both the design and implementation of laws designed to protect the public health and welfare. Congress is already starting to require agencies to provide more and better information about regulatory decisions. Given today's political climate, a larger role for economic analysis may not be possible. I hope, however, that as the public increasingly understands the importance of regulation, lawmakers will respond by allowing economics to play a more prominent role in the regulatory process. If Congress helps agencies to target social regulation more effectively, Americans will continue to enjoy a high standard of living and know that their government is able to tackle the nation's most important social problems. If Congress continues to allow agencies to create regulations without adequate attention to the full economic consequences, the standard of living that most citizens enjoy will slowly but surely erode. I offer my simple reform agenda in the hope of engaging legislators and policymakers interested in taking constructive action to improve the regulatory process.

4

The Internationalization of Regulatory Reform

Throughout the world, regulatory policy is undergoing sweeping reevalua-tion and reform. The purpose of this concluding chapter is to show how regulation and regulatory reform are becoming "internationalized." The internationalization of regulation has two dimensions. First, regulatory reform in different countries around the world has many common features. Second, regulation in certain areas is increasingly likely to be subject to international negotiations and oversight by transnational bodies. For example, domestic regulatory policies are receiving greater consideration in negotiations about international trade agreements, a development that shows that as the world economy moves toward freer trade, the indirect trade barriers created by regulation can become more significant than tar-iffs and quotas in distorting trade. I identify several areas in which those trends are emerging, particularly the regulation of the environment, finan-cial transactions, and regulatory trade barriers. I also offer political and economic rationales for the internationalization of regulation. After identi-fying three important factors affecting the structure of regulatory reform, I describe the nature of reforms we can expect to see in the coming decades and offer conclusions about the future of regulatory reform worldwide.

Important Factors Affecting the Structure of Regulatory Reform

Factors such as interest-group politics affect the structure of specific regulatory reforms.[1] Yet, I choose not to highlight interest-group politics here because scholars widely appreciate its role and because other critical factors affect the overall structure of regulatory reform. Three key factors particularly important for the kinds of regulation addressed in this book are globalization, wealth creation, and an improved understanding of the effects of regulation.

Globalization. By *globalization* I mean specific changes in technology that have led to lower costs of computing, communication, and transportation.[2] The world is simply a lot "smaller" than it used to be. It is easier to connect people around the globe for business and pleasure because the costs of communication and transportation have decreased dramatically.[3] With a single keystroke on my computer, I can send an electronic message halfway around the globe, and with a few keystrokes financiers can transfer huge amounts of capital across national boundaries.

Several authors have written about the general effects of globalization.[4] My interest here is somewhat narrower. I wish to focus on how the decline in the costs of computing, communication, and transportation are likely to affect regulatory reform and the structure of regulatory institutions.

The likely impact of globalization on regulation is complicated because globalization is likely to affect the structure of regulation, which in turn will influence the degree of globalization. For example, if globalization encourages telecommunications deregulation, that will stimulate innovation and thus further reduce the costs of communication. Despite the complicated effects of globalization on regulation, I can identify some of the more pronounced impacts. Globalization will affect the structure of regulation in different ways. While globalization may reduce the extent of economic regulation, it could stimulate the demand for social regulation.

The standard claim analysts of globalization make is that it will increase factor mobility.[5] Clearly, globalization has substantially increased capital mobility, but labor has also been affected. Lower transport and communication costs mean that one can easily sell and market services internationally. Such increased mobility is likely to have profound effects on the structure of markets. The geographic size of markets is growing as a result of the decrease in the costs of doing business across national boundaries.[6] One factor that limits the ability of governments to regulate business in certain ways is that some firms can contract out or relocate production and services to low-cost regions.[7] The increased threat of relocation or bypass means that countries will face pressures to reform outdated aspects of regulatory structures that keep prices above marginal costs. We already see reforms in several countries in sectors including financial services, telecommunications, energy, and transportation. Factor mobility is by no means the only explanation for the increased interest in economic regulatory reform, but it is certainly a key factor.

Not only have the costs of communication decreased, but the rate at which new information is broadcast to the world has increased. Those two trends create what we may think of as the "Cable News Network effect,"[8] which affects the spread of culture and many other important aspects of our life, such as the kinds of economic systems in which individuals function. Faster dissemination of information requires both government and business firms to respond more quickly to crises where the public clamors for regulation. Examples of that include the *Exxon Valdez* oil spill, mad cow disease, and the TWA flight 800 crash.

The trends resulting from globalization will make it more costly for governments to impose controls on labor, environment, products, and businesses. That is only part of a larger story, however.

We can expect the increase in factor mobility to limit the ability of governments to tax and spend and to inflate their currencies. The short-term response of markets to government actions will increasingly discipline both fiscal and monetary policy. Indeed, to the extent that fiscal and monetary policies are constrained, regulation will become a *relatively* more attractive tool for accomplishing social goals and redistributing wealth to preferred constituents.[9] That is, although the political cost of using all those instruments for redistributing wealth will increase with globalization, the political cost of using social regulation will increase less than the others since the costs of regulation are less visible than taxing and spending. For such regulation to transfer wealth effectively, policymakers must impose on it factors of production that are relatively immobile; otherwise, firms and individuals will be able to bypass the government's attempts to raise revenues and transfer wealth.[10]

Reduced costs of communication will also make it easier for groups to organize around international causes and to exploit the Cable News Network effect.[11] Groups with relatively modest levels of resources will be able to compete more effectively with large businesses in the political marketplace. In effect, the evolving technology will change the relative power of interest groups; environmental groups stand to gain from those changes more than business. For example, groups interested in international environmental problems such as climate change will find it easier to organize and further their objectives. They will increasingly use the media along with new and existing international institutions to achieve those objectives. We see that, for example, in recent efforts to develop a consensus for moving forward on an international agreement to reduce greenhouse gas emissions. We also see attempts to develop agreements that harmonize labor standards and environmental standards across countries.[12]

In short, globalization will increase the economic welfare of less regulated countries and thereby encourage further economic deregulation and privatization. At the same time, globalization does not imply the end of such regulation. In contrast, globalization is likely to encourage more social regulation since it will help make such regulation a more attractive tool for redistributing wealth. In the case of social regulation, however, some forces unleashed by globalization will also impede its growth to some extent by increasing its cost.

Changes in Wealth. The world is becoming a wealthier place on average, although great disparities in rates of GNP growth per capita exist among countries and regions. World GDP grew 1.8 percent per year between 1990 and 1994, and GNP per capita increased .9 percent per year between 1985 and 1994.[13] Despite the disparities, the general trend toward increased wealth in absolute terms and average per capita terms is indisputable.[14]

The increase in wealth is likely to increase demands on the government to help provide services that are viewed as "luxury" goods, such as environmental quality, workplace protection, and consumer protection. In addition, as countries become wealthier, more resources become available to governments to implement and enforce those policies to protect social welfare. Thus, we can expect to see a rise in that kind of regulation.[15] I consider below the precise form that such regulation will take.

Improved Understanding of the Effects of Regulation. A fundamental factor affecting the change in regulatory institutions is the change in our understanding of the impacts of regulation.[16] For example, airline deregulation in the United States developed in part from a natural experiment in which observers found unregulated fares within states to be substantially lower than regulated fares on comparable routes between states.[17] Indeed, analysts now widely accept that the regulation of prices, entry, or both in industries that are workably competitive is likely to result in net losses in economic well-being for the average person.

Similarly, analysts now widely recognize that the state has the important role of providing certain kinds of services that may limit such negative externalities as pollution. Analysts also recognize that government may have a role to play in providing information that may be difficult for firms or individuals to obtain, such as in the case of emerging technologies that could limit pollution without adversely affecting product and service quality.

Finally, analysts are more widely appreciating the limitations of government intervention, particularly at the federal level. First, the state is susceptible to political pressures that lead it to produce inefficient results. Second, federal intervention can be heavy-handed when the problems that need to be addressed are local in nature.

A large body of literature written over the past three decades identifies the conditions under which state intervention is likely to be effective, the kinds of state intervention that are likely to be effective, and the conditions for effective change.[18] That literature guides countries interested in reforming various aspects of their economies.[19]

The change in our understanding of political and economic institutions along with the increased rate at which information spreads has encouraged developing countries to explore new institutional arrangements for regulating their economies. Most prominently, developed and developing countries, including the countries in Eastern Europe, are rethinking the role of state-owned enterprises in their economies. Most countries show a steady trend away from such enterprises.[20]

Whither Regulatory Reform?

After examining some general themes in the future of regulatory reform, I focus on economic regulation, social regulation, and process regulation. In addition, I consider specific aspects of regulation related to labor markets. Finally, I address some international aspects of regulatory reform that are likely to become more important.

General Themes in Regulatory Reform. Two important related themes are emerging in the analysis of regulation and its reform. First, economic analysis should play a more prominent role. A wide spectrum of economists has argued that benefit-cost analysis and cost-effectiveness analysis should play a more prominent role in developing environmental, health, and safety regulations as well as other business regulations.[21] Academic economists still hotly debate the limits of the usefulness of that tool, but few disagree that it is a worthwhile mechanism for holding legislators and civil servants more accountable for their decisions. That tool is also useful for informing the decisionmaking process about the likely impacts of policies on the average citizen. To the extent that administrators become more accountable for the costs and benefits they impose on consumers, the greater use of such analysis could lead to more efficient and effective policy. As chapter 2 notes, the shift toward using economic analysis that considers costs as well as benefits in developing and implementing regulations is expanding, particularly in the United States, Australia, the United Kingdom, and Mexico.

A second important theme is that we should systematize the economic information compiled on regulations in a form that is readily available to interest groups. Indeed, an emerging consensus is that accounting for the impacts of government's regulatory activities is useful and desirable.[22] For example, in 1996 Congress required the director of the Office of Management and Budget to submit a report to Congress that provides "estimates of the total annual costs and benefits of Federal regulatory programs" and estimates of the costs and benefits of individual regulations.[23] That is the first statute that requires an accounting of the benefits and costs of federal regulation. As noted in chapter 2, similar efforts are underway in other countries.

Two factors have provoked the call for greater regulatory accountability: the unprecedented growth of federal regulatory activity since 1970—including environmental, health, and safety rules, employer mandates, and administrative paperwork burdens—and the increasing concern that the public is not getting its money's worth from regulation. Many scholars have shown that designing better rules could produce better regulatory results at a lower cost.[24]

The Future of Economic Regulation. We are likely to see less economic regulation in both developed and developing countries. That trend will result partly from globalization and partly from a deeper understanding of the impacts of economic regulation, which are usually adverse for the average citizen. In addition, the trends toward globalization cause new interest groups to support deregulatory efforts. Low-cost firms with new technologies can pose a potent challenge to existing incumbents in helping to deregulate key sectors of the economy. As low-cost firms enter new markets, incumbents will be forced to compete or leave.

Economic deregulation will generally happen in the developed countries first and gradually diffuse to the developing countries. The exceptions to that observation include Chile and some East European countries, which have accomplished much deregulation, and Japan, which has not. Nonetheless, diffusion will primarily proceed from developed to developing countries because the developed countries already have the institutional capability and the experience with sophisticated markets. Moreover, many developing countries are in the initial phases of privatizing their state-owned enterprises. As the process evolves, those nations will need to address more directly the precise forms of regulation they wish to use in the economic sphere.

As economic deregulation becomes more prominent, competition policy will become increasingly vigorous. Several countries already deregulating industries, such as Argentina, are attempting to develop competitive policies in conjunction with their deregulation and privatization efforts.[25] Those policies are particularly important in relatively small countries where single firms can dominate a market and exert significant influence over the political process. Without sensible competition policies, one may end up trading a regulated entity for an unfettered monopoly. If countries allow entry by foreign competitors, however, extensions in the geographic scope of markets will help to ensure robust competition.

A major question for economic deregulation is how far it can reach. For example, the politics and economics get more difficult as industries with network characteristics undergo deregulation.[26] A central question is the extent to which deregulation of the distribution sector for network industries would increase efficiency.[27] Some scholars assert that distribution in such industries as telecommunications, natural gas, and electricity is a natural monopoly.[28] Other scholars contend that deregulating distribution would generate major benefits, even if doing so creates some redundancy.[29] Indeed, consumers in many areas already enjoy the benefits of a variety of supermarkets and other retailers. Many distribution systems will become deregulated as changes in technology progressively weaken the natural monopoly argument for that part of the economic system. Cable television operators are already able to compete with telephone companies for a wide array of services to consumers and businesses.[30]

Where regulation remains, the use of incentive regulation such as price caps, which limit a firm's price increases instead of attempting to limit profits or rate of return directly, is likely to increase. Because firms may retain profits gained through cost reduction, incentive regulation motivates firms to minimize costs. Increasingly, U.S. federal and state regulators and U.K. regulators have used that approach for telecommunications as well as for electricity, water, and gas.[31]

The Future of Social Regulation. As I noted above, social regulation is likely to increase, particularly as societies become wealthier. But what form will that increase take? I begin by sketching a consensus that is forming in the United States. That consensus has four key elements. The first two are increasing the use of economic analysis and developing more systematic information on the benefits and costs of regulation, measures I have already discussed. The second two elements are no backsliding—allowing no reductions in improvements the public has gained from social regulation—and focusing on alternatives to traditional regulation. The consensus applies broadly to environmental, health, and safety regulation. I rely on the U.S. experience to build my case because the United States is in the vanguard in developing that consensus.

With respect to no backsliding, the public has made it clear in polls that a majority would be willing to sacrifice some economic growth for environmental quality.[32] Any politician who endorsed lowering government requirements for environmental protection, consumer protection, or worker safety would be committing political suicide. Lest politicians violate their obligation to protect the public, they must assert that they cannot and will not backslide. Thus, no rollback in such social regulation is acceptable. Indeed, we must continue to make progress on all fronts.

What does *no backsliding* mean? First, it requires defining and measuring the status quo in terms of the impact of social regulation. More important, it requires defining improvements to the status quo. Environmental groups, among others, have tended to adopt a very narrow definition of what improving the status quo means. They sometimes argue that a policy improves the status quo if and only if they can show that it improves every measurable characteristic about which they are concerned. The problem with such an approach is that one almost always has to make trade-offs, even within a narrow set of environmental characteristics. The extent to which policymakers can achieve substantial gains in environmental, health, and safety at a reasonable cost will depend critically on the nature of how one defines the status quo and improvements to the status quo.[33]

The final element in the consensus is a greater focus on alternatives to regulation that achieve social objectives more effectively. The idea of smarter regulation has been around for some time now.[34] It is hard to oppose more flexible, effective, and innovative regulation. Thus, such reform is a centerpiece of the National Performance Review initiated by President Clinton[35] as well as of the regulatory reforms touted in the Bush administration.[36] Although the actual outcomes are not clear, examples of such potential "win-win" programs include markets for controlling pollution and markets for allocating water. Those and other more flexible approaches could allow industry to develop innovative alternatives for worker safety, consumer protection, and environmental protection that can beat the status quo.

Related to the search for regulatory alternatives is a greater interest in eliminating policy instruments such as tax credits for ethanol production, below-cost timber sales, subsidies for oil production, and price supports or quotas for farm commodities that can lead to the overuse of resources. Thus, in 1996 Congress passed a farm bill that significantly reduced the outlays for commodity programs.[37]

Other forms of innovation may not increase the welfare of the average citizen. All Western countries are likely to place greater emphasis on product recycling,[38] although the economic and environmental value of such recycling is questionable in many cases.[39] In addition, greater emphasis is likely on product labeling for both food content and environmental impacts. The focus on certain kinds of efficiency standards is likely to continue.

Many of those regulations will decrease the economic well-being of the average consumer.

A major issue in social regulation is the kind of screening required for such new products as drugs and medical devices. The United States has shown positive trends by levying user fees to speed up the Food and Drug Administration's drug application reviews. On the other hand, the process for clinical testing of drugs has become increasingly cumbersome. In addition, the scope of regulation is expanding as new technologies including software for medical equipment become regulated. Furthermore, some argue that the FDA is increasingly regulating the medical practice by imposing rigid restrictions on the use of medical devices.[40]

How far politicians will move toward innovative regulation that focuses more on performance and outcome and less on process is unclear. But new approaches to regulation are certainly receiving much more serious consideration as the political and economic costs of social regulation become more apparent.

To suggest that social regulation is changing in positive ways does not imply that it will not be subject to such traditional forces as interest-group politics. For example, policymakers will still use social regulation to preserve jobs in some cases, to enhance the position of incumbent firms at the expense of new entrants, and to serve as an alternative to the budget when budgetary constraints are tight. Nonetheless, the forces outlined above are likely to play a dramatic role in the transformation of social regulation.

The Future of Process Regulation. We can think of process regulation—the government's management of the operation of the public and private sectors by imposing paperwork requirements and administrative costs that both producers and consumers must incur—as a separate category of regulation, but we can also think of such regulation as an important part of other economic and social regulation. Process regulation is likely to increase in some countries and sectors and to decrease in others. For example, firms will generally have to provide more information about their environmental activities. At the same time, several countries and individual states are reviewing existing and new regulations to make them more user-friendly while achieving the same or better social outcomes. Part of that user-friendliness will involve cutting red tape. Technology could help reduce such red tape, for example, through automated tax filings. In many sectors and countries, the trend toward reducing process regulation is likely to take place slowly—sometimes one regulation at a time. The problem is that many interest groups gain from having significant administrative burdens that add to the complexity of the process. In addition, process regulation can be a vehicle for corruption by creating opportunities for bribery, especially in developing and transition economies.

The Future of Labor Market Regulation. Changes in labor market regulation are likely to affect productivity and employment in the developed countries. While such regulation is only one element that affects the flexibility of the market, it is an important one.[41]

Part of the increase in social regulation, broadly defined, is likely to affect labor markets in the United States. In particular, employer mandates for medical insurance, mental health care, child care, and parental leave are likely. Periodic increases in the minimum wage are also likely. Those changes will make the U.S. labor market less flexible and will tend to reduce wages and in some cases employment.

In contrast, countries with heavily regulated labor markets, such as those in Western Europe, will experience some relaxation in labor market restrictions as the political costs of those restrictions begin to increase dramatically. Countries such as France, Germany, and Japan will introduce more flexibility in their labor market structure to increase their productivity and in the case of Western Europe to reduce current problems with high levels of unemployment, especially as the adoption of a common currency may aggravate those problems. In contrast, some developing countries may restrict the hiring of child labor to address political concerns about the use of that labor. The extent to which nations can and will enforce such rules is an open question.

International Aspects of Regulatory Reform

Some dramatic changes in regulatory reform at the international level or at least at the supranational level are likely. As economies become more interdependent through globalization and the reduction of trade restrictions, making greater use of international agreements and institutions to reconcile the need to regulate becomes more important. For example, the North American Free Trade Agreement stipulates specific requirements for labor and the environment for Mexico, Canada, and the United States. Here, I focus on two aspects of regulatory reform that are international or at least transnational in scope—free trade with the move toward harmonization and the perceived need to address externalities at a global level.

Free Trade and Harmonization. As trade restrictions are relaxed, individual countries are likely to make increasing use of regulation as a nontariff trade barrier.[42] Examples include the European Community's ban on hormone-fed beef and U.S. rules on reformulated gasoline that the World Trade Organization has determined discriminate against foreign oil refiners. Blocking those efforts at a domestic level is difficult because well-organized interest groups can maintain support for the policies. If nations can address questions of regulation and trade at a higher level, such as through the WTO, competing interests may be able to neutralize each other and thus develop more efficient policies.[43] Moving the locus of decisionmaking power from the national level to an international body such as the WTO will be a difficult political challenge. One way is to quantify the costs of those nontariff barriers to average consumers. A second is to show that often the primary purpose of those barriers is to prevent consumers from getting less expensive, higher quality products. Whether that information is sufficient to induce change is doubtful, but we can expect other interest groups, such as firms that may not enter new markets, to support the move. Those firms often provide a potent force for market and trade liberalization.

Increasingly, harmonization of standards has taken a prominent position in trade negotiations. The arguments for and against harmonization of different kinds of standards are well known.[44] When advanced industrial countries with similar standards harmonize them, such harmonization can constitute a free-trade, procompetition policy that decreases costs and increases welfare. On the other hand, the call for harmonization of standards can stem from interests in maintaining a status quo distribution of wealth. In some cases incumbent firms will seek harmonization toward tougher standards to preserve strategic advantage and thus will create entry barriers in global markets. Firms frequently use that strategy in domestic markets to raise the costs of particular groups of firms.

Harmonization of standards can reduce costs for producers in some cases. For example, rather than face different emission requirements in each country or state, automobile producers could reduce their costs by manufacturing a single type of vehicle that would meet all standards. On the other hand, alternatives to harmonization can achieve potentially greater cost savings for countries with similar standards. The United States and the European Union, for example, have drafted a mutual recognition agreement that would result, if signed, in automatic acceptance of each other's product standards in a variety of industries, including pharmaceuticals and telecommunications equipment.[45]

Harmonization can, of course, also raise the costs of production, if the developing world must meet the same labor and environmental standards as are currently applied in the United States and other developed countries. More agreements in which harmonization of certain kinds of product, labor, and environmental standards will play an important role are likely. Examples include agreements with less developed countries—such as with Mexico under the North American Free Trade Agreement—that coerce them into more strictly enforcing labor and environmental standards in exchange for freer trade.[46]

Harmonization can increase efficiency by limiting the tendency of governments to subsidize domestic firms, decreasing production costs, and reducing protectionist regulations within countries.[47] In the case of harmonizing labor and environmental standards between developed and developing countries, excessive levels of regulation could reduce the well-being of the average citizen in some developing countries.[48] In any case, we should generally analyze the impact of harmonization policies on a case-by-case basis.

Addressing Externalities at a Global Level. More international agreements to deal with global externality problems[49] are likely, particularly with respect to the environment.[50] Specific candidates for new international agreements include climate change and biodiversity. The emergence of an environmental agency that parallels the World Trade Organization is also possible but unlikely in the short term.[51]

The idea of shifting national policy to an international arena can, but need not, increase the well-being of the average citizen. Esty, for example, argues that we need a global environmental organization to address externality problems associated with environmental issues that existing regulations and institutions do not adequately address.[52] My view is that environmental interest groups that would not balance trade-offs to improve the overall well-being of the average citizen would likely capture such an organization. We must very carefully study the political economy of making policy changes to understand better how those changes will actually affect policy outcomes.

In addition to addressing environmental issues, nations may establish an international body or agreement to deal with problems in monitoring financial transactions across boundaries. The Bank of International Settlements, for example, has already established the Basel Accord, an international agreement requiring uniform minimum capital standards for commercial banks in signatory counties.[53] The trend toward expanding international oversight and regulation of financial transactions could be counterproductive if countries were to adopt those international standards without carefully analyzing their impacts.[54]

The changes in the international arena are not likely to be smooth. Some will enhance economic efficiency, while others will not. We can expect transnational bodies that deal with perceived externality problems related to regulation to emerge slowly.

Conclusion

This chapter has argued that regulation is likely to change dramatically in the years ahead. This book has laid out a framework for understanding some of the changes that are taking place as well as for suggesting how to improve current approaches to regulation.

We can no longer discuss regulatory reform in a purely domestic context because changes in the structure of global politics and global markets affect reform. Nor can we view regulation in isolation from other instruments of policy, such as legal instruments, taxation, monetary policy, trade, and international agreements.[55]

Great momentum exists to reform some aspects of the regulatory process—not just in the United States but throughout the world. A basic thesis of this chapter is that regulation and its reform are becoming *internationalized*. The movement toward regulatory reform will not be smooth. Moreover, it will exhibit certain characteristics of a diffusion process, with the developing countries' typically following the developed countries.

The forces underlying changes in regulation are likely to be quite potent. Specifically, I have argued that changes in globalization, increases in average wealth, and a deeper understanding of the impacts of regulation can help provide important clues about the future of regulation.

In general, that future is an optimistic one. Governments are learning to develop regulatory institutions that are better suited to their economic and social needs. The news is not all good from an economic standpoint, but the general directions of change are quite positive. Economic deregulation, partial deregulation, and privatization of specific industries are likely to create net gains for the average citizen. Although those trends will produce both winners and losers, the general impact on wealth creation will be quite positive. The picture is less clear for social and process regulations, although I am optimistic about them as well.

In the future we are likely to see more economic deregulation. As the political costs of regulating specific sectors of the economy increase, politicians will see deregulation as a cost-effective strategy for promoting growth. If other things are equal, we can expect countries with the greatest likely economic and political gains to proceed the most rapidly. We can expect policymakers to deregulate industries with a more complicated economic structure, such as electricity and telecommunications, more slowly.[56] Increased economic deregulation is likely to improve the economic well-being of the average citizen.

The future is also likely to increase the level of social regulation and change its form. In the United States an emerging consensus on social regulation could have important implications for domestic and international reform. We are likely to see more economic analysis of the impacts of regulation and a move toward more flexible approaches for implementation. Those changes will provide significant advantages for the average citizen. On the other hand, the demand for social regulation is likely to increase in the future. If that trend increases the level of burdensome regulations, the result could decrease the average citizen's well-being.

Process regulation will exhibit different patterns in different countries, and its impact on consumers and businesses will vary. Similarly, changes in labor market regulation will vary across countries. The United States will probably become less flexible as a result of mandates, and Europe will probably become more flexible in response to economic pressures. In general, more flexibility will improve productivity and output.

Finally, international institutions and agreements will play an increased role in addressing regulation and in imposing greater pressures to harmonize regulations. Those trends' impacts on economic efficiency will be highly dependent on the specific agreements and institutions that evolve.

In fifty years the United States is likely to see the virtual end of economic regulation, a sensible reduction in process regulation, and a more judicious approach to social regulation. Ever the optimist (along with Dr. Pangloss), I only hope that I can be here to observe whether my version of the future reflects the emerging reality.

Notes

Chapter 1: Reviving Regulatory Reform

1. See Noll (1999).
2. See Nivola (1997).
3. The barrier affected imports of gasoline from several sources, principally Venezuela. See World Trade Organization (1996).
4. See, for example, Lee and McKenzie (1991).
5. See Viscusi (1996).
6. See McGovern (1992).
7. See Guasch and Hahn (1999).
8. See Hahn et al. (2000).
9. See Morgenstern (1997).
10. See Winston and Morrison (1998).
11. See Howard (1995).
12. See Hahn and Hird (1991, 251). Unless otherwise stated, all dollar estimates in this chapter are in the year dollars of the cited publication.
13. See Winston (1993, 1284).
14. Mandates placed on business are also defined as social regulation. See chapter 2 for more details.

    Hahn and Hird (1991) suggest that the total benefits and costs of social regulation are comparable in 1988. They note, however, that large uncertainties exist in both the benefit and cost estimates. The annual costs of social regulation are estimated to range from $95 billion to $130 billion, while annual benefits range from $51 billion to $220 billion.
15. See Hahn (1996, 225–26) and Portney (1990).
16. See chapter 3 for more information about rules passing a benefit-cost test.
17. See chapter 2 for a normative discussion of the role of government in regulation.
18. See Arrow et al. (1996).

Chapter 2: Regulation and Its Reform around the World

1. See Hahn (2000a).
2. All estimates presented in this chapter are expressed in the year dollars of the original study.
3. See MacAvoy (1992).
4. For example, electronic mail will be more useful to a user if more people have e-mail addresses. On the subject of the economics of networks, see Katz and Shapiro (1991), Liebowitz and Margolis (1994), Klein (1996), and White (1999).
5. See Lewis (1996).
6. See Portney (1982).
7. See, for example, Weidenbaum and DeFina (1978), Litan and Nordhaus (1983), Hahn and Hird (1991), Hopkins (1992), and Winston (1993).
8. See Hahn and Hird (1991).
9. The efficiency costs of economic regulation were estimated to range from $45.3 billion to $46.5 billion, while economic transfers were estimated at $172.1 billion to $209.5 billion. The annual costs of social regulation were estimated to range from $78.0 billion to $107.1 billion; the annual monetized benefits ranged from $41.9 billion to 181.5 billion.
10. See Hopkins (1992).
11. Hopkins's estimate for the total cost of regulation includes transfer costs. Total costs without transfer costs are $412 billion.
12. Some studies do not count compliance as a regulatory cost. See Office of Management and Budget (1998).
13. See Winston (1993).
14. Consumers had annual gains of $32 billion to $43 billion per year from lower prices and better services, while producers gained about $3 billion per year from increased efficiency and lower costs.
15. See Winston (1998).
16. See, for example, Goklany (1992), Tengs and Graham (1996), and Hahn (1996).
17. See Anderson et al. (1997).
18. See Hahn (1996).
19. See Hahn (2000b) for updated estimates.
20. The estimates are not exhaustive, as not all sectors of the economy or all aspects of regulation are included. Thus, we should view the estimates as a lower bound on total regulatory costs.
21. The magnitude and even the direction of that impact are debated in the literature. See, for example, Jaffe et al. (1995), Hazilla and Kopp (1990), Jorgensen and Wilcoxen (1990), Gray (1987), Porter (1991), and Morgenstern (1997).
22. The estimates are often quite crude. For example, on the basis of an assumed ratio between private compliance costs and regulatory program spending, Mihlar (1996) extrapolated national regulatory costs in Canada

from federal and provincial administrative budgets. In addition, many of the estimates, especially the projections of benefits from deregulation in selected countries, are based on large macroeconomic models of the economy. It is dubious whether those models adequately capture the structural changes that would result from deregulation. Furthermore, the timing of those benefits is often unclear. Finally, the reforms that provide the basis for some of the modeling exercises may not be completely regulatory in nature. For example, Organization for Economic Cooperation and Development (1997a) describes the potential benefits of Japan's reforms as based on reducing the price and productivity gap with the United States, which regulatory differences in the two countries may only partly explain.

23. See Fundación de Investigaciones Económicas Latinoamericanas (1991).

24. The Organization for Economic Cooperation and Development (1997a) also used a macroeconomic model that suggested that regulatory reform programs could increase GDP in the long run by as much as 3.5 percent in the United Kingdom and by as much as 6 percent in Japan, Germany, and France.

25. The literature documenting the welfare gains of privatizing state-owned enterprises in both developed and developing countries is growing. See, for example, Galal et al. (1994). Those gains appear to be substantial in many cases. For example, in an examination of twelve cases of public enterprise divestiture, Galal et al. (1994) found that the annual component of the welfare gains averaged 30 percent of predivestiture annual sales and was positive in all but one of the cases.

26. See, for example, Kwoka (1996), Guasch and Hahn (1997), and Guasch and Spiller (1997).

27. See Evans et al. (1996).

28. For example, Nambu (1995) estimated that consumer surplus in Japan increased ¥245 billion (1993 yen) in 1993 as a result of privatization and deregulation of the telecommunications industry. Organization for Economic Cooperation and Development (1996a) reported that deregulation of the airline industry in Australia resulted in annualized net welfare gains of around $100 million. In the cases of Australia and New Zealand, the welfare gains may be attributable to privatization as well as to deregulation.

29. Several studies of the costs and benefits of certain pollution programs have been completed in developing countries, such as Chile and China. See World Bank (1994), Dasgupta et al. (1996), and Dasgupta et al. (1997).

30. Only a few countries, such as the United States, France, and the Netherlands, include private household expenditures related to abatement devices for motor vehicle emissions. In recent years those expenditures represent up to 10 percent of total pollution abatement expenditures.

31. See, for example, Joskow and Noll (1981).

32. See my discussion in the section "Recent Attempts at Reforming the Regulatory Process."

33. See Hoj, Kato, and Pilat (1996).
34. Those sectors accounted for 12 percent of U.S. GDP in 1985. See OECD (1997a).
35. See OECD (1992).
36. Regulation of that sector includes restrictions on shop operating hours and zoning laws that prohibit the location of large stores in certain areas.
37. The categorization of regulatory status is often quite subjective. OECD (1992) compiled it on the basis of surveys of selected countries. Furthermore, the national regulatory indicators—regulated, partly regulated, and unregulated—gloss over significant variation across countries and do not reflect conditions at the provincial, state, or local levels.
38. The airline sector is a good illustration of that pattern. The United States was the first to initiate major deregulatory efforts with the passage of the Airline Deregulation Act in 1978. Other OECD countries, such as Australia, Canada, New Zealand, and the United Kingdom, took major steps to deregulate and, in some cases, to privatize that sector in the last part of the 1980s. While complete privatization occurred in Japan in 1987, and some privatization occurred in continental Europe over that time period, the airline sectors in those countries remain partially regulated.
39. See World Bank (1995).
40. Although not addressed in this section, there is also a trend toward privatization and liberalization in European and Central Asian transition economies. See, for example, World Bank (1996).
41. See Galal et al. (1994), Levy and Spiller (1996), and Guasch and Spiller (1997).
42. See Grubb and Wells (1993).
43. See OECD (1995).
44. For example, Grubb and Wells (1993) calculate the summary indicator of employee work restrictions by summing three variables—protection of regular workers against dismissal, regulation of fixed-term contracts, and restrictions on overtime flexible weekend and night work—and effectively weighing each variable equally. The authors do not report the effect of different weighing schemes.
45. See, for example, Eisner (1997).
46. See, for example, Lazear (1990), Bean (1994), Koedijk and Kremers (1996), and Guasch (1997). In a study of eleven OECD countries, Koedijk and Kremers constructed an index of regulatory intensity in the countries and showed a sharp negative correlation between regulatory intensity and output growth. The countries with the least regulation enjoyed the highest growth in output per person. While the index was partly based on measures of labor market strictness, product market regulation was believed to have a greater influence on the findings. The measures the authors construct are admittedly crude but probably serve as a proxy for the degree to which markets are

regulated in different countries. Guasch has also argued that a correlation exists between labor market restrictions and employment growth. Thus, while many other factors can affect employment growth, we have strong reasons to believe that flexible labor market policies are likely to increase employment.

47. For example, the Family and Medical Leave Act of 1993 and the Health Insurance Portability and Accountability Act of 1996 increased mandated benefits to employees regarding child and health care, respectively.

48. See, for example, Evans et al. (1996) and Campos and Root (1996).

49. See, for example, OECD (1997a).

50. See Hopkins (1992).

51. See Office of Management and Budget (1996b) and Hahn (2000b). OIRA has estimated that the incremental annual costs of major final rules have exceeded $2 billion (1994 dollars) in each year since 1987. In two of the years, the annual costs exceeded $10 billion.

52. Identifying trends in the growth of regulation depends to some extent on the method of estimation. For example, we can examine costs in constant dollars or as a percentage of GDP. Likewise, we can estimate costs as annual expenditures or annualized over a relevant time frame. When examined in real terms, capital and operating expenditures for pollution abatement and control have generally increased since the 1980s. That trend is especially apparent when those costs are annualized because capital investments, often resulting from specific mandates, can be quite variable over time. The pattern of growth is not so clear when examining those expenditures as a percentage of GDP. For the most part, expenditures appear to grow at the same rate as or slightly faster than GDP.

53. See my discussion in the section "Recent Attempts at Reforming the Regulatory Process."

54. See Hahn (1996, 2000b).

55. See, for example, Hahn and Stavins (1991), Menell (1991), and OECD (1995).

56. For example, sunsetting clauses, in which all rules automatically expire within a specified time horizon unless remade through the normal rulemaking process, would be classified as "continuous."

57. No attempt has been made to examine how those requirements are actually enforced. Thus, the actual implementation may vary from that described in the table.

58. The extent to which public disclosure is allowed or required also varies from country to country.

59. Tables 2-4 and 2-5 do not include the Government Performance and Results Act of 1993. How that act will affect regulatory reform is unclear.

60. See National Association on Administrative Rules Review (1996). In addition, over half the respondents indicated that they considered whether the benefits of a rule outweighed the costs when reviewing rules.

Chapter 3: Regulatory Reform: Assessing the U.S. Government's Numbers

1. See Goldstein (1996).
2. See Howard (1995).
3. The study builds on my earlier work, a study of ninety-two environmental, health, and safety regulations from 1990 to mid-1996, and is part of a continuing project to track the costs and benefits of federal regulation. I added seventy-six regulations to the original database, some from 1981 to 1990 and some from 1995 to 1996. In the database, 115 rules are from the Environmental Protection Agency, 28 from the Department of Labor, 13 from the Department of Transportation, 5 from the Department of Health and Human Services, 4 from the Department of Agriculture, 2 from the Department of Housing and Urban Development, and 1 from the Consumer Product Safety Commission. My original analysis did not include the last three agencies. This study also covers operating agencies within the DOT not included in the original analysis, such as the Federal Aviation Administration, the Federal Railroad Administration, and the Research and Special Programs Administration. The original study only included the National Highway, Traffic, and Safety Administration. See Hahn (1996) for more information about the original study.
4. Agencies have produced RIAs for every regulation since Reagan's Executive Order 12291, issued in 1981. An RIA includes the agency's estimates of the benefits and costs of the regulation in addition to other information designated in the executive order. Reagan's order required agencies to produce an RIA for each proposed and final "major" rule, defined generally as a rule with an estimated annual impact on the economy of $100 million or more. President Clinton's Executive Order 12866, issued in 1993, changed the term *regulatory impact analysis* to *economic analysis* and the term *major* to *economically significant* but otherwise did not significantly change the RIA requirement. I use *regulatory impact analysis* throughout this chapter because analysts use the term more frequently than *economic analysis*. Clinton's order also changed the requirement that the benefits of a regulation must "outweigh" the costs to a requirement that the benefits of a regulation must "justify" the costs. The Clinton executive order also places more emphasis on the distributional impacts of regulations. Clinton intended the change in terminology to increase the weight attached to unquantifiable benefits and costs in agency analyses, but whether that change occurred is unclear. The impact of the two orders on the regulatory process differs, not because of subtle substantive variation, but because the Reagan administration and the Clinton administration implemented the orders very differently. The Clinton administration, for example, focused more on cooperation with the agencies.
5. The preamble often clarifies how the agency will implement the regulation and thus sheds light on the likely benefits and costs. I use the words *rule* and *regulation* interchangeably in this chapter.

6. I was not able to calculate net benefits, cost-effectiveness, and benefit-cost ratios for some rules in the database because the agencies did not provide sufficient information to complete those calculations.

7. Air pollution reduction benefits are from reduction in ambient levels of carbon monoxide, hydrocarbons, nitrogen dioxide, particulate matter, and sulfur dioxide.

8. See, for example, Weidenbaum and DeFina (1978), Litan and Nordhaus (1983), Morrall (1986), Hahn and Hird (1991), Hopkins (1992), Winston (1993, 1998), and Lutter and Morrall (1994).

9. See, for example, Breyer (1993) and Weidenbaum (1997).

10. For a description of regulatory reform efforts since Nixon, see Hahn (1998a).

11. Clinton's Executive Order 12866, which builds on Reagan's executive order, requires agencies to include the following information in an RIA: a statement of the potential need for the proposal, an examination of alternative approaches, an assessment of benefits and costs, the rationale for choosing the regulatory action, and a statement of statutory authority.

12. Grubb, Whittington, and Humphrey (1984) examined all RIAs prepared in 1981 and attempted to determine whether the requirements of Executive Order 12291 had improved regulatory outcomes. The General Accounting Office (1984) reviewed three Environmental Protection Agency analyses and made several recommendations to the agency to improve future analyses for rulemaking. In response to the GAO's recommendations, the Environmental Protection Agency (1987a) evaluated sixteen RIAs prepared in the first five years after Reagan issued Executive Order 12291. After briefly summarizing each analysis and subsequent regulatory decision, the EPA discussed the strengths and weaknesses of the analyses and outlined ways to improve their usefulness. The Office of Management and Budget (1988) evaluated nine RIAs from five different agencies on the basis of several criteria including: whether the analysis discussed market failure, evaluated suitable alternatives, reasonably treated uncertainty, clearly stated the baseline, and appropriately used discounting. In related work Fraas (1991) and Luken and Fraas (1993) reviewed the U.S. experience in using economic analysis to develop environmental policy. The authors noted tremendous variation in the quality and role of the analyses and then highlighted three well-prepared EPA RIAs that were important in the policy process. McGarity (1991) reviewed five RIAs from four agencies with a detailed examination of bureaucratic processes associated with regulatory development. Goodstein (1995), examining two RIAs in detail, sought to answer whether the EPA was producing good analyses and whether the analyses influenced decisionmaking. Rusin et al. (1996) evaluated six EPA RIAs and one Occupational Safety and Health Administration RIA. The authors determined whether each RIA discussed the need for regulatory activity, evaluated possible alternatives, estimated benefits and costs, and provided a rationale for choosing the proposed action. In the most com-

prehensive review of individual RIAs to date, Morgenstern (1997) examined the role of economic analysis in environmental decisionmaking. In that study separate authors evaluated twelve EPA RIAs. The authors focused on estimated impacts and the value of RIAs in regulatory decisions.

13. The General Accounting Office (1997, 1998, 1999) has conducted three additional studies that support those conclusions.

14. See Hahn (1996). While industry has an incentive to overstate costs in materials it provides to the agency, the agency has some discretion to determine which cost estimates to use. See Harrington, Morgenstern, and Nelson (1999) for an alternative perspective. While they find that costs are overstated in many cases, they also find that the assumed level of compliance is overstated. Thus, the bias in cost estimates is less clear for any given level of compliance. See also Office of Management and Budget (1998) for a discussion of that issue.

15. I base the benefit and cost numbers developed throughout this chapter on agency analyses, many of which are incomplete. Nonetheless, the numbers summarize the official information that is publicly available.

16. Agencies often differentiate between a rule's compliance costs and cost savings. Cost savings generally take the form of avoided costs of cleanup, property damage, resource replacement, litigation, and training in addition to savings from waste minimization, productivity gains, fuel economy benefits, and savings based on the value of lost product (for example, from oil spills). I combine cost savings and benefits in this analysis, although economists generally believe that most estimates of cost savings are implausible. Cost savings imply that regulations can save companies money and therefore that some companies are not maximizing profits. In my database, for example, including cost savings leads to ten regulations that save money. In addition, cost savings are difficult to estimate and are probably much smaller than agencies predict. See Porter and van der Linde (1995) and Palmer, Oates, and Portney (1995) for discussions of cost savings.

17. I define health benefits as those resulting from reducing the risk of cancer, heart disease, and lead poisoning. Safety benefits are those resulting from reducing the risk of disabling injuries, injuries that require a person to miss work, and injuries that do not require a person to miss work. Disabling injuries are permanent, and all other injuries are temporary. The injuries result from car, fire, and workplace accidents or the malfunction of consumer products.

18. Rules addressing safety risks estimate the benefits from reducing mortality and morbidity in all but two cases. In contrast, rules addressing health and environmental risks estimate those benefits about half the time. Note that all agencies, except for the DOL, are not distinguished by the type of regulatory risks they address. My analysis of the DOT, for example, includes ten safety rules as well as three U.S. Coast Guard rules aimed at preventing oil pollution in the health and environment category.

19. OSHA is a part of the DOL. I divided the DOL regulations in my database into health and safety categories because of the large number of rules in

each of those categories relative to other agencies. All DOL health regulations referred to throughout this chapter are OSHA health regulations. DOL safety regulations are OSHA safety regulations and Mine Safety and Health Administration regulations.

20. Examples include a rule assessing the extent to which general federal actions conform to state or federal implementation plans under the Clean Air Act, a rule outlining the operating permits program of that act, and a rule describing data requirements for pesticide registration. The EPA only qualitatively described the benefits of those rules.

21. The database primarily consists of "major" and "economically significant" regulations, as defined by Reagan's and Clinton's executive orders. It includes a few rules that may not be considered major in their final form, but I evaluated them on the presumption that they could be major. Although the CPSC is not covered by the executive orders, I included one rule from the CPSC that probably would have been designated as "major" if it was subject to review. I also reviewed rules from the Nuclear Regulatory Commission, which voluntarily complies with many executive order requirements.

22. See Hahn (1996, 216–19).

23. The terminology is somewhat misleading and has led to unnecessary controversy. Economists are trying to measure what people are willing to pay for small changes in the probability of reducing different kinds of health and safety risks, not the value of saving a life.

24. See Viscusi (1993).

25. Unless otherwise noted, I updated all estimates to 1995 dollars by using implicit price deflators for the gross domestic product from Council of Economic Advisers (1997).

26. See National Highway Traffic Safety Administration and Federal Highway Administration (1991) and Viscusi (1992).

27. I did not include disease and injury benefits that did not fit into fatality index categories, and I therefore may have understated benefits. Examples include reductions in diseases unique to only one or a few regulations, such as the incidence of reduced IQ levels as a result of lead exposure. When agencies monetized those benefits, I included agency valuations in an alternative scenario. While aggregate benefits increase by less than 5 percent, including those nonstandardized benefits is significant in a few rulemakings. For example, a 1992 Health Care Financing Administration rule addressing clinical laboratory improvements had annual costs of over $1 billion in selected years. Using a willingness-to-pay model for improved laboratory conditions and information on the cost of false negatives and positives, HCFA determined that the benefits ranged from $.5 billion to $5 billion annually. The agency did not specify the year dollars in the rule, but presumably the estimates are in 1991 or 1992 year dollars. As I am skeptical of some of those numbers, I include them only in an alternative scenario.

28. I did not take the estimates of the benefits of pollution reduction directly from any particular study. I based the estimates on a review of a variety of studies, the most important of which are Harrison et al. (1992), Rowe et al. (1995), and the EPA's RIA for municipal waste combustors (Environmental Protection Agency 1994). I believe that the final estimates represent a reasonable range of estimates. Al McGartland of the EPA reviewed those estimates and offered valuable feedback, but he is in no way responsible for the final choice of estimates. More refined estimates would take into account the level of pollution, population density, and differences in seasonal effects.

29. The net benefits estimate for final rules does not include two rules on stratospheric ozone (included in table 3-1) that the EPA asserts produce net benefits in trillions of dollars. I excluded those rules here because, while they may have positive net benefits, the EPA's estimates probably overstate the actual benefits significantly. For a detailed analysis of the EPA's aggregate estimates of clean air benefits, see Lutter (1998).

30. Sixty final regulations in the database have negative net benefits, while forty-six regulations have positive net benefits. Of the proposed regulations, seventeen have negative net benefits, and thirteen have positive net benefits.

31. Table 3-4 distinguishes between gross costs and net costs because, as discussed earlier in this chapter, agencies frequently distinguish between compliance costs and cost savings resulting from a rule. Gross costs are direct compliance costs. Net costs represent the difference between gross costs and any cost savings or additional costs associated with the rule. I compute net benefits as benefits minus net costs.

32. I excluded rules from the net benefits calculation in three circumstances. First, I excluded general rules that overlapped specific regulatory requirements. The EPA, for example, sets goals for the concentration levels of criteria pollutants but separately promulgates rules to ensure compliance with those standards. Second, I excluded a few rules for which the basis for the estimates was unclear. I may eventually enter those rules in the database. Finally, I excluded seventeen rules that I determined the agency was unlikely to finalize. Seven of those rules are related to the EPA's benzene standards, proposed in 1989 and 1990. The seven benzene decisions were part of a bundle of eleven benzene decisions promulgated by the EPA in two major rules, although I treated each of them as a separate data point. I left the other four benzene decisions in the database.

33. The estimates of benefits and costs in the RIAs of proposed rules are not so robust as the estimates for final rules because agencies often significantly change their estimates between the proposed and final stages of the rulemaking process, in response to OMB comments and for other unknown reasons. Agencies also never finalize some proposed rules. In addition, the year of implementation for proposed rules is unknown, a factor that makes the timing of the benefits and costs difficult to estimate. I therefore attach

more significance to the results of my analysis of the final rules, although analysis of the proposed rules reveals some interesting patterns.

34. HHS rules show positive net benefits, however, when nonstandardized, monetized benefits are included. HHS net benefits are negative because of HCFA rules with negative net benefits. The net benefits of Food and Drug Administration rules are positive.

35. All agencies except the DOT have positive net benefits for proposed rules with nonstandardized, monetized benefits.

36. The two FIFRA regulations are a 1992 rule setting worker protection standards for agricultural pesticides and a 1982 rule outlining data requirements for pesticide registration. The four TSCA regulations are a 1989 rule pertaining to the manufacture, importation, processing, and distribution of asbestos, a 1987 rule pertaining to materials that contain asbestos in schools, a 1985 rule pertaining to the manufacture, processing, and distribution of polychlorinated biphenyls (PCBs), and a 1983 rule outlining premanufacture notification and review procedures.

37. See Hahn (1996).

38. Thirty rules with net costs did not clearly quantify any benefits that I monetized for my calculations.

39. In general, as the discount rate increases, future costs and benefits are valued less. If benefits occur further in the future than costs, which is generally the case, net benefits should also decrease. The opposite should hold true when the discount rate is decreased. In this calculation, however, certain components of health benefits actually increase in value with higher discount rates. Thus, the net benefits of a rule can increase or decrease with changes in the discount rate, which is what I observe here.

40. The exceptions are 1982, 1983, 1986, 1987, and 1996. The values are much smaller than the positive values of other years.

41. We can draw the intuition by evaluating a set of positive cash flows over time, say from 1980 to 2010. First, take the present value of that stream (analogous to a base year of 1980). As the discount rate increases, the present value goes down because each component of the benefit stream decreases in value. Next, consider a future value of that stream in 2010 (analogous to a base year of 2010). By the same logic, each component increases with an increase in the discount rate. Finally, a base year in between 1980 and 2010 increases some early values in the stream and reduces later values. The impact of varying the discount rate requires making further assumptions about the nature of the benefit stream.

42. Another measure, frequently used in environmental regulation, is the cost per ton of pollutant reduction. The measure is typically used for Clean Air Act regulations. I use the cost-per-life-saved measure because it applies to a broader class of regulations in the database. Neither measure includes some of the benefits from ecosystem protection that agencies cannot easily quantify.

43. President Carter created OIRA with the Paperwork Reduction Act of 1980,

but the act was not implemented until the end of 1980. For the purpose of the analysis, I therefore assumed that OIRA was created January 1, 1981. Before Reagan introduced the RIA requirement in 1981, data on the benefits and costs of regulations were sparse. As a result, the Hahn-Morrall data set contains estimates for only ten rules from the period 1967 to 1980, while we have estimates for seventy-one rules from 1981 to 1995.

44. To calculate the cost-effectiveness of regulations, I use a methodology similar to that of Morrall (1986), Tengs and Graham (1996), and Tengs et al. (1994). I define costs as direct, or gross, costs. I define effectiveness in terms of "adjusted" lives and life-years. Lives and life-years are adjusted to account for significant nonfatal diseases and injuries by using the fatality index discussed in my earlier work. I compute cost-effectiveness by dividing the annualized cost by the annualized lives or life-years saved as a result of the regulation. I use "life-years" instead of "lives" because life-years better account for the effect of a premature death or variation in the number of years an individual must live with the consequences of a nonfatal injury or disease. For example, the use of life-years accounts for the fact that a child has more years of life remaining than an elderly person. The discount rate for the base case is 5 percent.

45. As with the calculation of the net benefits discussed earlier in this chapter, modification of key parameters can significantly affect cost-effectiveness estimates and therefore the results of the analysis. My cost-effectiveness estimates do not appear sensitive to changes in key parameters. Changes in the parameters did not result in differences greater than an order of magnitude. The sensitivity analysis also did not modify the relative ranking of rules based on the estimates of cost-effectiveness.

46. I base that estimate on data from 1993. The gross national product estimate is from Council of Economic Advisers (1997), and I adjusted it to 1995 dollars. The number of deaths from both cancer and accidents are from U.S. National Center for Health Statistics (1995). I assume that 2 percent of cancer deaths are induced by environmental causes (Ames and Gold 1996).

47. Seven of the rules that would not pass are regulations from the Resource Conservation and Recovery Act.

48. See, for example, Goklany (1992), Morrall (1986), Tengs and Graham (1996), and Hahn (1996).

49. I further discuss the benefit-cost ratio regression in the following section.

50. See Morrall (1986) and Lutter and Morrall (1994). I evaluated fifty-two final regulations, and Morrall evaluated twenty-nine final regulations. Before pooling those regulations, I tested for structural stability between the Hahn data and the Morrall data by applying the Chow test. I could not reject the null hypothesis that the two regressions are the same. Hence, pooling the data is reasonable. The regulations represent only a fraction of the regulations evaluated by Hahn and Morrall, who respectively evaluated 144 and 47 final regulations. But the regulations used in the regression are the

only ones for which it was possible to calculate cost-effectiveness, because the agency did not estimate benefits for a large number of the regulations and thus made the calculation of cost-effectiveness impossible. Eighteen regulations overlapped between Hahn's database and Morrall's database. For the Hahn-Morrall pooled regression, I used the Hahn estimates for the overlapping regulations. Of the overlapping eighteen regulations, four of the cost-effectiveness estimates differed by more that an order of magnitude. I believe that the difference results from Morrall's adjustments to the agency's numbers, because I took the agency's numbers as given. Morrall adjusted the agency numbers on the basis of a detailed analysis of specific rules to correct agency errors (Morrall 1986). I ran a regression with Morrall's estimates for the overlapping regulations, and the results of the regression did not change. My cost-effectiveness analysis has an advantage over Morrall's analysis because a third party can more easily reproduce it.

51. I initially used the value for cost-effectiveness, but none of the results was significant. The logarithmic function narrows the range on cost-effectiveness and provided a better fit to the data.

52. The Hahn-Morrall pooled regression uses cost per life saved because the cost per life-year saved data are not available for the Morrall estimates.

53. Because this analysis contains only final rules, it has thirteen fewer observations than the Hahn-Morrall pooled regression in Hahn (1996), which included proposed and rejected rules. I decided to use only final rules because the agency's estimates of the benefits and costs may change significantly between proposed and final rules and because agencies may never finalize some proposed rules. For example, the agency did not take final action on eleven of the proposed rules I reviewed. A general examination of those rules suggests that as the cost-effectiveness of a rule increases, it is less likely an agency will take final action on that rule. The basis for an agency's decision not to take final action is often unclear, however, and it is possible that poor cost-effectiveness is not the primary reason. I am hesitant to attribute such agency decisions to enlightened agency behavior or effective OIRA oversight as Viscusi (1996) suggests. The EPA, for example, withdrew a 1992 proposed rule to revise a program related to enhanced monitoring requirements for vehicles although the rule was relatively cost-effective. It is possible that other factors influence an agency's decision not to take action, but identification of those factors was beyond the scope of my study. Moreover, the number of no-action rules I examined is small and comprises primarily a series of EPA rules to reduce health risk from benzene in 1989 and 1990. It is difficult to draw defensible conclusions from such a small sample. To test the influence of proposed rules, I included proposed rules for which agencies provided estimates in the Hahn and the Hahn-Morrall pooled regressions. The explanatory power of the model decreased as a result of including proposed rules. I also included a dummy variable for proposed rules in both regressions. The dummy variable was not significant in either model.

54. The original purpose of OIRA was to improve the efficiency and effectiveness of government operations, including review of proposed regulations eventually expanded the review responsibilities of OIRA to include review of regulatory impact analyses of proposed and draft final rules.

55. Morrall's data include some minor rules as well as some regulations before the development of formal RIAs, while the Hahn data include only "major" regulations and "economically significant" regulations, as defined by Reagan's Executive Order 12291 and Clinton's Executive Order 12866.

56. Public perception of risk and its influence on agency priorities has been extensively discussed in the literature. See, for example, Slovic, Fischoff, and Lichtenstein (1985), Viscusi and Magat (1987), and Sunstein (1996).

57. Noncancer rules in the database are primarily regulations pertaining to health risk resulting from lead poisoning and poor nutrition. Those regulations are widely regarded as relatively cost-effective compared with other regulations.

58. That finding excludes one HUD safety rule addressing improved wind standards for manufactured housing. The cost-effectiveness of the rule is approximately one-fourth that of the median EPA regulation. Although that rule ranks poorly in terms of its cost-effectiveness, it actually results in net cost savings when the agency considers extensive property damage losses. Therefore, I do not include the rule in that comparison.

59. Of thirty-three total EPA regulations in the database, twenty-nine are cancer regulations. Forty of the eighty-one total regulations in the database are cancer regulations.

60. A coefficient is "marginally significant" if it is significant at the 10 percent level when using a two-tailed t-test, "significant" if it is significant at the 5 percent level, and "highly significant" if it is significant at the 1 percent level.

61. The interpretation of that and other regression coefficients is based on the conversion of the coefficients from the natural logarithm. The range is based on a calculation of a 95 percent confidence interval.

62. To measure whether EPA cancer regulations are less cost-effective than other cancer regulations, I included an interaction variable for the EPA and cancer in the original regression. Because the EPA-cancer variable and the cancer variable are highly correlated (the correlation coefficient = .75), however, I expected some instability in the model. I was somewhat surprised that the EPA-cancer variable was marginally significant in the Hahn-Morrall pooled regression. The EPA-cancer variable was highly significant in a regression that did not include the cancer variable, however. In addition, the EPA-cancer variable was statistically significant in the Hahn regression. The standard errors of both the EPA-cancer variable and the cancer variable in both the Hahn and the Hahn-Morrall pooled regressions increase relative to regressions in which only one of the variables is included. That probably results from the collinearity.

63. Again, the range is calculated on the basis of a 95 percent confidence interval.

64. In addition, the data may be biased. The data set could include, for example, EPA regulations that are among the most cost-effective of all EPA rules because the EPA did not quantify the costs and benefits of less cost-effective rules. Alternatively, some EPA rules that are very cost-effective may not be in the database because the EPA promulgated them before Reagan's executive order required agencies to submit information on the benefits and costs of regulations.

65. The results of the regression on Morrall's complete data set, described in Hahn (1996), are similar to the results of the Hahn and the Hahn-Morrall pooled regressions. In the 1996 Morrall regression, the cancer variable is significant, and the EPA variable is insignificant, although the year variable is significant.

66. I present the regression with the OIRA variable only to stimulate discussion about how to measure its impact quantitatively. The OIRA variable and the year variable are highly correlated (correlation coefficient = −.77); as a result, the model is unstable. I believe that the instability makes the year variable in the model significant.

67. The OIRA variable was not significant in any specification of the model presented in this chapter, including a model in which the only independent variables were the cancer variable and the OIRA variable. I also tried to capture the impact of the RIA requirement in Reagan's Executive Order 12291 and Clinton's Executive Order 12866. I created dummy variables for each order. According to my results, neither order significantly affected cost-effectiveness estimates. The result is probably also related to the lack of observations before 1981, however.

68. The pattern over time appears to be driven in part by the type of rules promulgated in a particular year. Specific agencies often prepare analyses with similar characteristics. All National Highway Traffic Safety Administration rules, for example, estimated health benefits but did not monetize those benefits, while all HHS rules estimated and monetized benefits and passed a benefit-cost test.

69. I also tested whether the political affiliation of the administration affected cost-effectiveness estimates, but no significant relationship exists. The result may be a function of the definition of the variable. Many rules developed under one administration are promulgated under a subsequent one, but I used the year of promulgation to link each regulation with a particular administration. The Clinton administration, for example, promulgated many of the rules associated with the 1990 Clean Air Act Amendments Congress passed during the Bush administration. I further tested the hypothesis that rules promulgated during election years are less cost-effective than other regulations, as believed by many diligent observers of the regulatory process, but my results indicate that the election year does not significantly affect cost-effectiveness. Again, that result may be a consequence of the limitations of the data. More work must be done to determine whether those variables affect regulatory efficiency.

70. See Environmental Protection Agency (1987b).
71. I included only air pollution reduction benefits because the agencies did not generally quantify any benefits from pollution reduction other than from air pollution reduction. According to the EPA, those benefits are large and may therefore significantly affect the results of the regression. Pollution reduction benefits can change the cost-effectiveness estimates by orders of magnitude and in some cases can even change the sign of the estimates. See Hahn (1996, 229) for details. My general valuation of air pollution reduction benefits affects the benefit-cost ratios of regulations with air pollution benefits, however, as discussed earlier in this chapter. Those benefits are subject to a great deal of uncertainty because of our incomplete understanding of the science and the difficulty of measuring society's willingness to pay for improvements in air quality. Moreover, the willingness-to-pay estimates could vary dramatically, depending on the level of pollution and the location.
72. I study fifty-two final rules with data on cost-effectiveness and net benefits. A comparison of the natural logarithms of the standard measures of cost-effectiveness and the benefit-cost ratio revealed a correlation of –.80 when costs savings are included in the measurement of the benefit-cost ratio and –.96 when cost savings are excluded. This suggests that the measures result in a relatively similar ranking of rules for that particular case.
73. The benefit-cost ratio regression contains the same fifty-two regulations for which Hahn-Siskin estimates of cost-effectiveness are also available. It further contains an additional fifty-three regulations, thirty-two of which have no quantified benefits and twenty-one of which have quantified benefits only from air pollution. I ran a regression using only the fifty-two regulations that were also used in the Hahn cost-effectiveness regression, and the results of my benefit-cost ratio regression did not change. The R^2 of the benefit-cost ratio regression with only 52 regulations increased from .18 to .31 relative to the regression with 105 regulations, however.
74. I transformed the logarithmic function by adding a small constant (.001) to include rules with no benefits or cost savings. Changing the size of the constant did not significantly affect my results.
75. As a result of the broad range of qualitative health benefits, the specification of many EPA rules into cancer and noncancer categories is difficult. The health variable includes all cancer regulations in addition to regulations that reduce the risk from lead poisoning and heart disease. A few rules do not clearly fit into either the health or the safety category. Examples include U.S. Coast Guard rules to reduce the frequency and severity of oil spills and USDA rules that address the treatment and care of animals. I dropped those rules from the regression.
76. Eliminating those regulations from the regression did not change the results.
77. Like the cost-effectiveness regressions, however, the EPA-health variable and the health variable are highly correlated (correlation coefficient = .71). Of the

eighty-four health regulations in the database, sixty-nine are EPA health regulations. Not surprisingly, the EPA-health variable is highly significant in a regression that excludes the health variable. The health variable is also highly significant in a regression that excludes the EPA-health variable.

78. See, for example, Magat, Krupnick, and Harrington (1986).

79. While the Clean Air Act prohibits the EPA from considering costs or welfare benefits when it sets primary national ambient air quality standards, the agency is required to consider such factors as technical feasibility, affordability, and cost-effectiveness in setting standards for motor vehicles and new or modified stationary sources.

80. See *Risk Assessment and Cost Benefit Act of 1995*, 104th Cong., 1st sess., H.R. 1022, and *Comprehensive Regulatory Reform Act of 1995*, 104th Cong., 1st sess., S. 343. The House version language is stronger.

81. For that categorization, I relied on Environmental Protection Agency (1987a), Fraas (1991), Rhomberg (1997), and Downing (1995).

82. In *International Union, UAW v. OSHA*, 938 F.2d 1310 (1991), the District of Columbia Circuit Court remanded OSHA's interpretation of the Occupational Safety and Health Act, which was restricted only by "feasibility," and suggested that benefit-cost analysis was consistent with the language of the act. Environmental Protection Agency (1987a) indicates that, while the Resource Conservation and Recovery Act is silent with regard to the appropriate consideration of costs, benefits and costs not related to human health and the environment should not be considered in rulemaking.

83. Since agencies are required by executive orders to estimate and, to the extent feasible, to quantify the benefits and costs of all major rules, I would not expect significant differences in the completeness of analyses.

84. On the basis of the rules reviewed in the regulatory scorecard, more than 60 percent of rules clearly fall into that category while an additional 18 percent of rules arguably would be placed in that category.

85. That result is probably driven by the fact that rules from statutes without limitations more frequently monetized benefits (48 percent versus 22 percent). The comparison is 48 percent versus 18 percent when OSHA-safety and Resource Conservation and Recovery Act rules are included in the "with limitations" category.

86. None of the rules authorized by the Federal Insecticide, Fungicide, and Rodenticide Act and the Toxic Substances Control Act—the two statutes that allow benefit-cost balancing—passes a benefit-cost test. Almost 18 percent of other EPA rules pass a benefit-cost test according to agency calculations.

87. The comparison is 50 percent versus 42 percent when OSHA-safety and Resource Conservation and Recovery Act rules are included in the "with limitations" category. In addition, when nonstandardized yet monetized benefits are included in the base case, the comparison is 59 percent versus 38 percent.

88. Provisions under the executive orders and the Unfunded Mandates Reform Act of 1995 require agencies to choose the least burdensome alternative to

a regulation or describe in the rulemaking record why the agency did not select the least burdensome alternative. Agencies are not required to quantify the efficiency losses from not choosing the least burdensome alternative, however. In addition, agencies sometimes choose the least burdensome alternative from a predefined set of alternatives that exclude potentially efficiency-enhancing approaches to regulation.

89. RIAs tend to have a greater impact on the process if they contain relatively complete estimates of benefits and costs and if agencies use the RIA information in the early stages of the rulemaking process. For example, scholars frequently refer to an EPA rule to reduce lead in gasoline as an RIA that influenced the agency's decision because it was thorough and well-prepared. See, for example, Fraas (1991). For a good study of several RIAs, see also Morgenstern (1997).

90. My analysis of the benefits and costs of regulations is based not only on the government's numbers but also on my assumptions concerning a discount rate and valuation of benefits. Since agencies used a variety of assumptions to estimate costs and benefits, it was necessary to use a consistent discount rate and consistent values for benefits to compare regulations and aggregate net benefits.

91. Five rules of the forty-four rules that pass a benefit-cost test with monetized benefits pass a benefit-cost test on the basis of net cost savings or monetized benefits. An additional three rules pass a benefit-cost test if I use the more favorable range of agency's calculations to estimate benefits and costs.

92. In assessing individual regulations, I view the values for pollution reduction used here as very rough approximations. For example, if many of the proposed emission reductions occur in areas that are already in compliance with the air quality standards, the values used in the base case probably overstate the benefits. One example where the benefits are likely to be overstated is for reductions in nitrogen oxide emissions in the Northeast.

93. The only exception to that observation is the number of Clean Air Act rules that pass a benefit-cost test with changes in the value of pollution reduction.

94. See Hahn (1996, 223–34).

95. The survey is designed to estimate the impact of future agency actions and to evaluate existing programs. Regulatory activities covered include major and minor rulemaking as well as other activities, such as licensing, enforcement, letters of opinion, administrative orders, and exemptions.

96. See Bliley (1997) and Furchtgott-Roth (1996).

97. The agencies include the Consumer Product Safety Commission, the Department of Commerce, the Department of Energy, the Department of Health and Human Services, the Environmental Protection Agency, the Federal Communications Commission, the Food and Drug Administration, the Federal Energy Regulatory Commission, the Federal Trade Commission, the Interstate Commerce Commission, the Nuclear Regulatory Commission, the Occupational Safety and Health Administration, the Securities and Exchange Commission, and the Surface Transportation Board.

98. See Nuclear Regulatory Commission (1995). Although primarily a law enforcement agency, the Federal Trade Commission has requirements in place to examine the projected benefits and any adverse economic effects of rules (Bliley 1997, 114). In addition, the Federal Energy Regulatory Commission has completed benefit-cost analyses of recent rules associated with the restructuring of the natural gas and electricity industries.
99. The Consumer Product Safety Commission and the Nuclear Regulatory Commission indicated, however, that they could calculate the total costs of their regulations to their agency, other government agencies, and the private sector (Bliley 1997).
100. See National Highway Traffic Safety Administration and Federal Highway Administration (1991).
101. See Environmental Protection Agency (1990, 1997). As discussed previously, those estimates are often incomplete and may be methodologically flawed and systematically biased. See, for example, Hahn (1996).
102. Most agencies probably have some information on the impact of their programs but have not compiled it because Congress or the White House does not require agencies to present such information to the public.
103. See Katzen (1994).
104. When the Government Performance and Results Act of 1993 is fully implemented, I may have more complete information to assess the effectiveness of agency review programs. Under the act, agencies are required to prepare strategic plans, comprehensive mission statements, and annual program evaluations.
105. See, for example, Arrow et al. (1996).
106. See, for example, Smith (1984), Arrow et al. (1996), and Graham and Wiener (1995, chap. 11).
107. For more detailed discussions of those improvements, see Arrow et al. (1996), Hahn (1996), and the Office of Management and Budget (1996a).
108. See, for example, Arrow et al. (1996) and Crandall et al. (1997).
109. See Hahn and Litan (1997).

Chapter 4: The Internationalization of Regulatory Reform

1. See Noll and Owen (1983).
2. My definition of *globalization* focuses on changes in technology and costs. Other writers have referred to it as the increasing interdependence of economies measured in terms of trade and capital mobility. See "The World Economy Survey" (1996, 4).
3. Within a decade or two, the price of ordinary telephone calls will not be sensitive to distance or duration. See "The Revolution Begins, At Last" (1995, 15).
4. See, for example, McKenzie and Lee (1991), Wriston (1992), and Garrett (1995).
5. See, for example, McKenzie and Lee (1991).
6. Globalization has the effect of dramatically expanding the scope of markets as well as competition in many cases. Those definitions need to be taken into account in devising sensible competition policies for different countries, as I note later. The lower transaction costs between units of a firm

could also have the effect of lowering the average firm size.

7. In addition, as regulations become easier to avoid, rules such as geographic restrictions and interest rate regulation of banks will increasingly hurt firms that previously benefited from those restrictions. See Kroszner and Strahan (1999).

8. The Gulf War provides a good example. The fact that Americans could watch the war in real time on television had profound implications for how the war was conducted. That capability will also affect how future wars are conducted (Glynn 1995). The key point is that the speed at which information travels will affect the range of options available to policymakers.

9. See Hahn (1990).

10. A similar argument can be made for the taxation of relatively immobile factors of production. Of course, there will be other considerations in tax policy, including politics and economic efficiency.

11. For example, advocacy groups such as the Natural Resources Defense Council conducted a successful media campaign in an attempt to ban the pesticide alar, a substance they argued posed serious carcinogenic risks, although the scientific basis for their claims was suspect. See Marshall (1991).

12. See Bhagwati (1996).

13. See World Bank (1996).

14. Although many of the 133 countries tracked by the World Bank show negative growth, at the regional level positive growth appears to be the norm (World Bank 1996).

15. High-income countries tend to have more stringent environmental regulations and stricter enforcement. In fact, studies have shown that, beyond a critical income level, countries show a decline in pollution as income increases. See Grossman and Krueger (1995) and World Bank (1992).

16. See Joskow and Noll (1981), Guasch and Hahn (1997), and Noll (1999).

17. See Levine (1965).

18. See, for example, Noll (1971), White (1981), Noll and Owen (1983), World Bank (1995), and Campos and Root (1996).

19. See, for example, Organization for Economic Cooperation and Development (1992) and Arrow et al. (1996).

20. See Galal et al. (1994) and World Bank (1995, 1996). To the extent that those countries adopt institutions that generate wealth and do so with some concern for the distribution of wealth, we can expect to see a greater demand for social regulation, as noted above.

21. See Arrow et al. (1996) and Crandall et al. (1997).

22. See Hahn and Litan (1997).

23. See the Omnibus Consolidated Appropriations Act of 1997.

24. See Morrall (1986), Tengs and Graham (1996), Viscusi (1996), and Anderson et al. (1997).

25. Although substantial differences exist in competition laws, most developed nations now have restrictions on price fixing and other anticompetitive behavior. See Scherer (1994).

26. See Noll (1999).

27. See Klein (1996).
28. See, for example, White (1999).
29. See Smith (1987, 1996).
30. See, for example, Crandall and Furchtgott-Roth (1996), Hazlett and Spitzer (1997), Vogelsang and Mitchell (1997), and White (1999).
31. See Sappington and Weisman (1996) and Armstrong, Cowan, and Vickers (1994).
32. See Ladd and Bowman (1995).
33. For example, taking lead out of gasoline resulted in higher benzene emissions from the new fuel. That naturally leads to comparison of the risks associated with the old fuel versus the new fuel. In the case of lead, the decision was made to remove it because the risks associated with the new fuel were thought to be significantly lower, and the costs were acceptable.
34. See Drayton (1981).
35. See Gore (1993).
36. See Bush (1989).
37. See Congressional Research Service (1996).
38. See Salzman (1997).
39. See Tierney (1996).
40. See Calfee (1997).
41. Other important factors include cultural norms, such as Japan's long-term employment model, and differences in the structure of collective bargaining.
42. Indeed, one can expect nations and states to attempt to shift costs to others outside their jurisdiction.
43. See Noll (1997). Moving the process to a higher level, however, is not in itself sufficient to guarantee a more efficient outcome. The key is to ensure that negotiations take place over a number of regulatory issues, so that competing interest groups will tend to cancel each other out, and the result will be lower regulatory and trade barriers.
44. See Leebron (1996).
45. See Coleman (1997).
46. To the extent that such welfare-reducing agreements are traded off in the political arena against possible welfare-enhancing agreements, such as freer trade, the total impact on welfare is difficult to predict.
47. See White (1996).
48. If important environmental spillover effects exist among countries, such as for the case of acid rain, nations may need to coordinate policies to achieve a more efficient solution.
49. Not all those problems will necessarily involve global externalities, but they often will be couched in those terms to argue for some form of centralized control.
50. See Hahn and Richards (1989) and Barrett (1994).
51. See Esty (1994).
52. See Esty (1994).
53. The Basel Committee on Banking Supervision established the Basel Capital

Accord in 1988. The accord was an agreement among the central banks of the G-10 countries to enforce a common minimum capital standard for commercial banks by 1992 (Basel Committee on Banking Supervision 1988).

54. The Basel standards, especially as proposed for modification in June 1999, may actually be counterproductive. For an extended analysis, see U.S. Shadow Financial Regulatory Committee (2000).

55. Indeed, in the short term the reforms examined here are likely to be highly contentious, thus leading to major legal battles in countries such as the United States, where the battles are typically fought out in the legislature and the courts.

56. See Noll (1999).

References

Ames, Bruce N., and Lois S. Gold. 1996. "The Causes and Prevention of Cancer: Gaining Perspectives on Management of Risk." In Robert W. Hahn, ed., *Risks, Costs, and Lives Saved: Getting Better Results from Regulation*. New York and Washington, D.C.: Oxford University Press and AEI Press.

Anderson, Robert, Alan Carlin, Al McGartland, and Jennifer Weinberger. 1997. "Cost Savings from the Use of Market Incentives for Pollution Control." In Richard Kosobud and Jennifer Zimmerman, eds., *Market-Based Approaches to Environmental Policy*. New York: Van Nostrand Reinhold.

Armstrong, Mark, Simon Cowan, and John Vickers. 1994. *Regulatory Reform: Economic Analysis and British Experience*. Cambridge: MIT Press.

Arrow, Kenneth J., Maureen L. Cropper, George C. Eads, Robert W. Hahn, Lester B. Lave, Roger G. Noll, Paul R. Portney, Milton Russell, Richard Schmalensee, V. Kerry Smith, and Robert N. Stavins. 1996. *Benefit-Cost Analysis in Environmental, Health, and Safety Regulation: A Statement of Principles*. Washington, D.C.: AEI Press.

Australia. 1986. "Review of Business Regulations." Information Paper No. 2. Department of Industry, Technology, and Commerce, Business Regulation Review Unit, Canberra, Australia.

Avery, B. 1997. Personal communication with author. Cabinet Office, Deregulation Unit, London, April 15.

Barrett, Scott. 1994. "Self-Enforcing International Environmental Agreements." *Oxford Economic Papers* 46: 878–93.

Basel Committee on Banking Supervision. 1988. *International Convergence of Capital Measurement and Capital Standards*. Basel: Bank of International Settlements.

Bean, Charles R. 1994. "European Unemployment: A Survey." *Journal of Economic Literature* 32 (2): 573–619.

Belconnen Industry Commission. 1995. *The Growth and Revenue Implications of*

Hilmer and Related Reforms. Final report. Belconnen ACT, Australia: Belconnen Industry Commission.

Bhagwati, Jagdish. 1996. "The Demands to Reduce Diversity among Trading Nations." In Jagdish Bhagwati and Robert E. Hudec, *Fair Trade and Harmonization: Prerequisite for Free Trade? Volume 1: Economic Analysis.* Cambridge: MIT Press.

Bliley, Thomas J., Jr. 1997. *Survey of Federal Agencies on Costs of Federal Regulations.* Staff report prepared for the Committee on Commerce, U.S. House of Representatives. Washington, D.C.: Government Printing Office.

Boles de Boer, David, and Lewis Evans. 1996. "The Economic Efficiency of Telecommunications in a Deregulated Market: The Case of New Zealand." *Economic Record* 72: 24–35.

Breyer, Stephen G. 1993. *Breaking the Vicious Circle: Toward Effective Risk Regulation.* Cambridge: Harvard University Press.

Bush, George. 1989. *Building a Better America.* Washington, D.C.: Government Printing Office.

Calfee, John E. 1997. "Regulating Medical Progress: The Growth of FDA Controls over Health Care Technology and Practice." Working paper, American Enterprise Institute, Washington, D.C.

Campos, José Edgardo, and Hilton L. Root. 1996. *The Key to the Asian Miracle: Making Shared Growth Credible.* Washington, D.C.: Brookings Institution.

Coleman, Brian. 1997. "U.S., EU Draft Pact on Trade-Product Standards." *Wall Street Journal,* May 29.

Congressional Research Service. 1996. "Farm Bill Issues: Overview." Congressional Research Service Report for Congress, IB 95058, June 6.

Council of Economic Advisers. 1995. *Economic Report of the President, 1995.* Washington, D.C.: Government Printing Office.

———. 1997. *Economic Report of the President, 1997.* Washington, D.C.: Government Printing Office.

Crandall, Robert W., and Harold Furchtgott-Roth. 1996. *Cable TV: Regulation or Competition?* Washington, D.C.: Brookings Institution.

Crandall, Robert W., Christopher DeMuth, Robert W. Hahn, Robert E. Litan, Pietro S. Nivola, and Paul R. Portney. 1997. *An Agenda for Federal Regulatory Reform.* Washington, D.C.: AEI Press and Brookings Institution Press.

Dasgupta, Susmita, Mainul Huq, David Wheeler, and Chonghua Zhang. 1996. "Water Pollution Abatement by Chinese Industry: Cost Estimates and Policy Implications." Policy Research Working Paper 1630. Washington, D.C.: World Bank, Environment, Infrastructure, and Agriculture Division.

Dasgupta, Susmita, Hua Wang, and David Wheeler. 1997. "Surviving Success: Policy Reform and the Future of Industrial Pollution in China." Policy Research Division, Environment, Infrastructure, and Agriculture. Washington, D.C.: World Bank.

Downing, Donna M. 1995. "Cost-Benefit Analysis and the 104th Congress: Regulatory Reform, 'Reg-icide,' or Business as Usual?" Master's thesis, George Washington University, National Law Center, Washington, D.C.

Drayton, William. 1981. "Getting Smarter about Regulation." *Harvard Business*

Review 59 (July/August): 38–52.

Eisner, Robert. 1997. "A French Lesson." *Wall Street Journal,* June 4.

Emerson, Michael, Michel Aujean, Michel Catinat, Philippe Goybet, and Alexis Jacquemin. 1992. *The Economics of 1992: The EC Commission's Assessment of the Economic Effects of Completing the Internal Market.* Oxford: Oxford University Press.

Environmental Protection Agency. 1987a. *EPA's Use of Benefit-Cost Analysis 1981– 1986.* Washington, D.C.: Government Printing Office.

———. 1987b. *Unfinished Business: A Comparative Assessment of Environmental Problems.* Washington, D.C.: Government Printing Office.

———. 1990. *Environmental Investments: The Cost of a Clean Environment.* EPA-230-11-90-083. Washington, D.C.: Government Printing Office.

———. 1994. *Economic Impact Analysis for Proposed Emission Standards and Guidelines for Municipal Waste Combustors.* EPA-450/3-91-029. Research Triangle Park, N.C.: Environmental Protection Agency.

———. 1997. *The Benefits and Costs of the Clean Air Act, 1970 to 1990.* Research Triangle Park, N.C.: Environmental Protection Agency.

Esty, Daniel C. 1994. *Greening the GATT: Trade, Environment, and the Future.* Washington, D.C.: Institute for International Studies.

Evans, Lewis, Arthur Grimes, Bryce Wilkinson, and David Teece. 1996. "Economic Reform in New Zealand 1984–95: The Pursuit of Efficiency." *Journal of Economic Literature* 34 (December): 1856–1902.

Fraas, Arthur. 1991. "The Role of Economic Analysis in Shaping Environmental Policy." *Law and Contemporary Problems* 54: 113–25.

Fundación de Investigaciones Económicas Latinoamericanas. 1991. *Regulatory Costs in Argentina.* Buenos Aires: Fundación de Investigaciones Económicas Latinoamericanas.

Furchtgott-Roth, Harold. 1996. "Neglect of Costs in Federal Regulation: Benign or Malignant?" Paper presented at conference, Regulatory Reform: Making Costs Count, December 9, at American Enterprise Institute, Washington, D.C.

Galal, Ahmed, Leroy Jones, Pankaj Tandon, and Ingo Vogelsang. 1994. *Welfare Consequences of Selling Public Enterprises: An Empirical Analysis.* Washington, D.C.: World Bank.

Garrett, Geoffrey M. 1995. "Capital Mobility, Trade, and the Domestic Politics of Economic Policy." *International Organization* 49 (4): 657–87.

General Accounting Office, General Government Division. 1997. "Regulatory Reform: Agencies' Efforts to Eliminate and Revise Rules Yield Mixed Results." GGD-98-3. Washington, D.C.: Government Printing Office.

———. 1999. "Regulatory Reform: Some Agencies' Claims Regarding Lack of Rulemaking Discretion Have Merit." GGD-99-20.Washington, D.C.: Government Printing Office.

General Accounting Office, Resources, Community, and Economic Development Division. 1984. "Benefit-Cost Analysis Can Be Useful in Assessing Environmental Regulations, Despite Limitations." RCED-84-62, April 6. Washington, D.C.: Government Printing Office.

———. 1998. "Regulatory Reform: Agencies Could Improve Development, Documentation, and Clarity of Regulatory Economic Analyses." RCED-98-142. Washington, D.C.: Government Printing Office.

Glynn, Patrick. 1995. "Quantum Leap: Parallelism between Quantum Mechanics and Politics." *National Interest* 39 (Spring): 50–57.

Goklany, Indur. 1992. "Rationing Health Care While Writing Blank Checks for Environmental Hazards." *Regulation* (Summer): 14–15.

Goldstein, Bernard D. 1996. "Risk Assessment as an Indicator for Decision Making." In Robert W. Hahn, ed., *Risks, Costs, and Lives Saved: Getting Better Results from Regulation.* New York and Washington, D.C.: Oxford University Press and AEI Press.

Goodstein, Eban. 1995. "Benefit-Cost Analysis at the EPA." *Journal of Socio-Economics* 24 (2): 375–89.

Gore, Al. 1993. *From Red Tape to Results: Creating a Government That Works Better and Costs Less.* Washington D.C.: Government Printing Office.

———. 1995. *Common Sense Government: Works Better and Costs Less.* Third report of the National Performance Review. Washington, D.C.: Government Printing Office.

———. 1996. *The Best Kept Secrets in Government: A Report to President Bill Clinton.* Washington, D.C.: Government Printing Office.

Graham, John, and Jonathan B. Wiener, eds. 1995. *Risk v. Risk: Tradeoffs in Protecting Health and the Environment.* Cambridge: Harvard University Press.

Gray, Wayne B. 1987. "The Cost of Regulation: OSHA, EPA, and the Productivity Slowdown." *American Economic Review* 77 (5): 998–1006.

Grossman, Gene M., and Alan B. Krueger. 1995. "Economic Growth and the Environment." *Quarterly Journal of Economics* 110 (2): 353–77.

Grubb, David, and William Wells. 1993. "Employment Regulation and Patterns of Work in EC Countries." OECD Economic Studies No. 21. Paris: OECD.

Grubb, W. Norton, Dale Whittington, and Michael Humphrey. 1984. "The Ambiguities of Benefit-Cost Analysis: An Evaluation of Regulatory Impact Analyses under Executive Order 12291." In V. Kerry Smith, ed., *Environmental Policy under Reagan's Executive Order: The Role of Benefit-Cost Analysis.* Chapel Hill: University of North Carolina Press.

Guasch, J. Luis. 1997. *Labor Reform and Job Creation: The Unfinished Agenda in Latin America and Caribbean Countries.* Directions in Development Series. Washington, D.C.: World Bank.

Guasch, J. Luis, and Robert W. Hahn. 1997. "The Costs and Benefits of Regulation: Some Implications for Developing Countries." World Bank Policy Research Working Paper 1773. Background paper for *World Development Report.* Washington, D.C.: World Bank.

———. 1999. "The Costs and Benefits of Regulation: Implications for Developing Countries." *World Bank Research Observer* 14: 137–58.

Guasch, J. Luis, and Pablo Spiller. 1997. *Managing the Regulatory Process: Design, Concepts, Issues, and the Latin America and Caribbean Story.* Directions in Development Series. Washington, D.C.: World Bank.

Hahn, Robert W. 1990. "Instrument Choice, Political Reform, and Economic Welfare." *Public Choice* 67: 243–56.

————. 1996. "Regulatory Reform: What Do the Government's Numbers Tell Us?" In Robert W. Hahn, ed., *Risks, Costs, and Lives Saved: Getting Better Results from Regulation.* New York and Washington, D.C.: Oxford University Press and AEI Press.

————. 1998a. "Government Analysis of the Benefits and Costs of Regulation." *Journal of Economic Perspectives* 12 (Fall): 201–10.

————. 1998b. "State and Federal Regulatory Reform: A Comparative Analysis." Working Paper 98-3. Washington, D.C.: AEI-Brookings Joint Center for Regulatory Studies. November.

————. 2000a. "The Internationalization of Regulatory Reform." In Robert W. Hahn, *Reviving Regulatory Reform: A Global Perspective.* Washington, D.C.: AEI Press.

————. 2000b. "Regulatory Reform: Assessing the Government's Numbers." In Robert W. Hahn, *Reviving Regulatory Reform: A Global Perspective.* Washington, D.C.: AEI Press.

Hahn, Robert W., and John Hird. 1991. "The Costs and Benefits of Regulation: Review and Synthesis." *Yale Journal on Regulation* 8 (Winter): 233–78.

Hahn, Robert W., and Robert E. Litan. 1997. *Improving Regulatory Accountability.* Washington, D.C.: AEI Press and Brookings Institution Press.

————. 1998. "An Analysis of the Second Government Draft Report on the Costs and Benefits of Federal Regulations." Working paper 98-1. Washington, D.C.: AEI-Brookings Joint Center for Regulatory Studies.

Hahn, Robert W., and Kenneth Richards. 1989. "The Internationalization of Environmental Regulation." *Harvard International Law Journal* 30 (Spring): 421–46.

Hahn, Robert W., and Robert N. Stavins. 1991. "Incentive-Based Environmental Regulation: A New Era from an Old Idea?" *Ecology Law Quarterly* 18 (1): 1–42.

Hahn, Robert W., Jason K. Burnett, Yee-Ho I. Chan, Elizabeth A. Mader, and Petrea R. Moyle. 2000. "Assessing Regulatory Impact Analyses: The Failure of Agencies to Comply with Executive Order 12866." *Harvard Journal of Law and Public Policy* 23 (3): 859–85.

Harrington, Winston, Richard D. Morgenstern, and Peter Nelson. 1999. "On the Accuracy of Regulatory Cost Estimates." Discussion paper 99-18. Washington, D.C.: Resources for the Future.

Harrison, David, Jr., Albert L. Nichols, John S. Evans, and Douglas J. Zona. 1992. *Valuation of Air Pollution Damages.* Cambridge: National Economic Research Associates.

Hazilla, Michael, and Raymond J. Kopp. 1990. "Social Cost of Environmental Quality Regulations: A General Equilibrium Analysis." *Journal of Political Economy* 98 (4): 853–73.

Hazlett, Thomas W., and Matthew L. Spitzer. 1997. *Public Policy toward Cable Television: The Economics of Rate Controls.* Cambridge and Washington, D.C.: MIT Press and AEI Press.

Hoj, Jens, Toshiyasu Kato, and Dirk Pilat. 1996. "Deregulation and Privatization in the Service Sector." OECD Economic Studies No. 25. Paris: OECD.

Hopkins, Thomas D. 1992. *Costs of Regulation: Filling the Gaps.* Report prepared for Regulatory Information Service Center, Washington, D.C.: Regulatory Information Service Center.

Howard, Philip K. 1995. *The Death of Common Sense: How Law Is Suffocating America.* New York: Random House.

Jaffe, Adam B., Steven R. Peterson, Paul R. Portney, and Robert N. Stavins. 1995. "Environmental Regulation and the Competitiveness of U.S. Manufacturing: What Does the Evidence Tell Us?" *Journal of Economic Literature* 33: 132–63.

Jorgenson, Dale W., and Peter J. Wilcoxen. 1990. "Environmental Regulation and U.S. Economic Growth." *RAND Journal of Economics* 21 (2): 314–40.

Joskow, Paul L., and Roger G. Noll. 1981. "Regulation in Theory and Practice: An Overview." In Gary Fromm, ed., *Studies in Public Regulation.* Cambridge: MIT Press.

Katz, Michael L., and Carl Shapiro. 1991. "Systems Competition and Network Effects." *Journal of Economic Perspectives* 8 (Spring): 93–115.

Katzen, Sally. 1994. "The First Year of Executive Order No. 12866." Office of Information and Regulatory Affairs, Office of Management and Budget, Washington, D.C.

Klein, Michael. 1996. "Competition in Network Industries." Policy Research Working Paper No. 1591. Washington, D.C.: World Bank, Private Sector Development Department. April.

Koedijk, Kees, and Jeroen Kremers. 1996. "Market Opening, Regulation, and Growth in Europe." *Economic Policy: A European Forum* 23 (October): 445–67.

Kroszner, Randall S., and Philip E. Strahan. 1999. "What Drives Deregulation?: Economics and Politics of the Relaxation of Bank Branching Restrictions." *Quarterly Journal of Economics* 114 (4): 1437–67.

Kwoka, John E. 1996. "Privatization, Deregulation, and Competition: A Survey of Effects on Economic Performance." Washington, D.C.: World Bank, Private Sector Development Department.

Ladd, Everett C., and Karlyn H. Bowman. 1995. *Attitudes toward the Environment: Twenty-five Years after Earth Day.* Washington, D.C.: AEI Press.

Lazear, Edward P. 1990. "Job Security Provisions and Empoyment." *Quarterly Journal of Economics* 105 (3): 699–726.

Leebron, David W. 1996. "Lying Down with Procrustes: An Analysis of Harmonization Claims." In Jagdish Bhagwati and Robert E. Hudec, eds., *Fair Trade and Harmonization: Prerequisite for Free Trade? Volume 1: Economic Analysis.* Cambridge: MIT Press.

Levine, Michael E. 1965. "Is Regulation Necessary? California Air Transportation and National Regulatory Policy." *Yale Law Journal* 74: 1416–47.

Levy, Brian, and Pablo Spiller. 1996. "A Framework for Resolving the Regulatory Problem." In Brian Levy and Pablo Spiller, eds., *Regulations, Institutions, and Commitment.* New York: Cambridge University Press, 1996.

Lewis, Tracy R. 1996. "Protecting the Environment When Costs and Benefits Are Privately Known." *RAND Journal of Economics* 27 (Winter): 819–47.

Liebowitz, S. J., and Stephen E. Margolis. 1994. "Network Externality: An Uncommon Tragedy." *Journal of Economic Perspectives* 8 (Spring): 133–50.

Lipschitz, Leslie, Jeroen Kremers, Thomas Mayer, and Donogh McDonal. 1989. "The Federal Republic of Germany: Adjustment in a Surplus Country." Occasional Paper No. 64, International Monetary Fund, Washington, D.C.

Litan, Robert E., and William D. Nordhaus. 1983. *Reforming Federal Regulation.*

New Haven: Yale University Press.

Luken, Ralph A., and Arthur G. Fraas. 1993. "The U.S. Regulatory Analysis Framework: A Review." *Oxford Review of Economic Policy* 9 (4): 100.

Lutter, Randall W. 1998. "An Analysis of the Use of EPA's Clean Air Benefit Estimates in OMB's Draft Report on the Costs and Benefits of Regulation." *Regulatory Analysis* 98-2. Washington, D.C.: AEI-Brookings Joint Center for Regulatory Studies.

Lutter, Randall W., and John F. Morrall III. 1994. "Health–Health Analysis: A New Way to Evaluate Health and Safety Regulations." *Journal of Risk and Uncertainty* 8: 43–66.

MacAvoy, Paul W. 1992. *Industry Regulation and the Performance of the American Economy.* New York: W. W. Norton.

Magat, Wesley, Alan Krupnick, and Winston Harrington. 1986. *Rules in the Making: A Statistical Analysis of Regulatory Agency Behavior.* Washington, D.C.: Resources for the Future.

Marshall, Elliott. 1991. "A Is for Apple, Alar, and . . . Alarmist?" *Science* 254 (October 4): 20–22.

Massachusetts Executive Office for Administration and Finance. 1996. "Regulation Review Project: The Implementation of Executive Order 384—To Reduce Unnecessary Regulatory Burden: An Interim Report." Boston: Massachusetts Executive Office for Administration and Finance.

McGarity, Thomas O. 1991. *Reinventing Rationality: The Role of Regulatory Analysis in the Federal Bureaucracy.* New York: Cambridge University Press.

McGovern, George. 1992. "Manager's Journal: A Politician's Dream Is a Businessman's Nightmare," *Wall Street Journal*, June 1.

McKenzie, Richard B., and Dwight R. Lee. 1991. *Quicksilver Capital: How the Rapid Movement of Wealth Has Changed the World.* New York: Free Press.

Menell, Peter S. 1991. "The Limitations of Legal Institutions for Addressing Environmental Risks." *Journal of Economic Perspectives* 5 (Summer): 93–113.

Mexico, Secretaria de Comercio y Fomento Industrial. 1997. *Economic Deregulation in Mexico.* Mexico City: Economic Deregulation Council.

Mihlar, Fazil. 1996. *Regulatory Overkill: The Costs of Regulation in Canada.* Vancouver, B.C.: Fraser Institute.

Morgenstern, Richard D., ed. 1997. *Economic Analysis at EPA: Assessing Regulatory Impact.* Washington, D.C.: Resources for the Future.

Morrall, John F. 1986. "A Review of the Record." *Regulation* 10 (November–December): 25–34.

Nambu, Tsuruhiko. 1995. "Competition and Regulation of Japanese Telecommunications Industry." Discussion Paper 62, Economic Research Institute, Economic Planning Agency, Tokyo, Japan.

National Association on Administrative Rules Review, Council of State Governments. 1996. *1996–1997: Administrative Rules Review—Directory and Survey.* Lombard, Ill.: Thompson Legal Publishing.

National Highway Traffic Safety Administration and Federal Highway Administration. 1991. *Moving America More Safely: An Analysis of the Risks of Highway Travel and the Benefits of Federal Highway, Traffic, and Motor Vehicle Safety Programs.* Washington, D.C.: Government Printing Office.

Nichols, Albert L. 1997. "Case Study: The RIA for the 1985 Lead-in-Gasoline Phasedown." In Richard D. Morgenstern, ed., *Economic Analysis at EPA: Assessing Regulatory Impact*. Washington, D.C.: Resources for the Future.

Nivola, Pietro, ed. 1997. *Comparative Disadvantages?: Social Regulations and the Global Economy*. Washington, D.C.: Brookings Institution Press.

Noll, Roger G. 1971. *Reforming Regulation: An Evaluation of the Ash Council Proposals*. Washington, D.C.: Brookings Institution.

————. 1997. "Internationalizing Regulatory Reform." In Pietro S. Nivola, ed., *Comparative Disadvantages?: Social Regulations and the Global Economy*. Washington, D.C.: Brookings Institution Press.

————. 1999. *The Economics and Politics of the Slowdown in Regulatory Reform*. Washington, D.C.: AEI-Brookings Joint Center for Regulatory Studies.

Noll, Roger G., and Bruce Owen. 1983. "The Political Economy of Deregulation: An Overview." In Roger Noll and Bruce Owen, eds., *The Political Economy of Deregulation*. Washington, D.C.: American Enterprise Institute.

Nuclear Regulatory Commission. 1995. *Regulatory Analysis Guidelines of the U.S. Nuclear Regulatory Commission*. Final report, NUREG/BR-0058, revision 2. Washington, D.C.: Government Printing Office.

Office of Management and Budget. 1988. *The Role of Regulatory Impact Analysis*. Regulatory Program of the United States Government, April 1, 1987–March 31, 1988. Washington, D.C.: Government Printing Office.

————. 1993. *Regulatory Program of the United States Government, April 1, 1992–March 31, 1993*. Washington, D.C.: Government Printing Office.

Office of Management and Budget, Office of Information and Regulatory Affairs. 1996a. *Economic Analysis of Federal Regulations under Executive Order No. 12866*. Washington, D.C.: Government Printing Office.

————. 1996b. *More Benefits, Fewer Burdens: Creating a Regulatory System That Works for the American People*. Washington, D.C.: Government Printing Office.

————. 1998. *Report to Congress on the Costs and Benefits of Federal Regulations*. Washington, D.C.: Government Printing Office.

Organization for Economic Cooperation and Development. 1992. *Regulatory Reform, Privatization, and Competition Policy*. Paris: OECD.

————. 1995. *Evaluating the Efficiency and Effectiveness of Economic Instruments: A Conceptual and Empirical Analysis*. ENVIRONMENTAL/EPOC/GEEI(95)16. Paris: OECD.

————. 1996a. *Regulatory Reform: A Country Study of Australia*. OCDE/GD(96)91. Paris: OECD.

————. 1996b. *Pollution Abatement and Control Expenditure in OECD Countries*. OCDE/GD(96)50. Paris: OECD.

————. 1996c. *Competition, Regulation, and Performance*. ECO/CPE/WP1(95)6. Paris: OECD.

————. 1997a. "The Economywide Effects of Regulatory Reform." Chap. 1 in *The OECD Report on Regulatory Reform, Volume 2: Thematic Studies*. Paris: OECD.

————. 1997b. "Regulatory Quality and Public Sector Reform." Chap. 2 in *The OECD Report on Regulatory Reform, Volume 2: Thematic Studies*. Paris: OECD.

Palmer, Karen, Wallace E. Oates, and Paul R. Portney. 1995. "Tightening Environmental Standards: The Benefit-Cost or the No-Cost Paradigm?" *Journal of Economic Perspectives* 9 (Fall): 119–32.

Porter, Michael E. 1991. "America's Green Strategy." *Scientific American* (April): 168.

Porter, Michael E., and Class van der Linde. 1995. "Toward a New Conception of the Environment-Competitiveness Relationship." *Journal of Economic Perspectives* 9 (Fall): 97–118.

Portney, Paul R. 1982. "How Not to Create a Job." *Regulation* (November/December): 35–38.

———. 1990. "Economics and the Clean Air Act." *Journal of Economic Perspectives* 4 (Fall): 173–81.

"The Revolution Begins, At Last." 1995. *Economist* 336 (September 30): 15–16.

Rhomberg, Lorenz. 1997. "Federal Agency Risk-Assessment and Risk-Management Practices." In Commission on Risk Assessment and Risk Management, *Risk Assessment and Risk Management in Regulatory Decision-Making*. Final report of the Commission on Risk Assessment and Risk Management, vol. 2. Washington, D.C.: Government Printing Office.

Rowe, Robert D., Lauraine G. Chestnut, Carolyn M. Lang, Stephen S. Bernow, and David E. White. 1995. *The New York Environmental Externalities Cost Study: Summary of Approach and Results*. Boulder, Colo.: RCG Hagler Bailly.

Rusin, Michael, Robert C. Anderson, Thomas J. Lareau, G. Prasad Rao, and Arthur Wiese. 1996. *Analysis of the Costs and Benefits of Regulation: A Review of Historical Experience*. Discussion paper no. 804R, Policy Analysis and Strategic Planning Department. Washington, D.C.: American Petroleum Institute.

Salzman, James. 1997. "Sustainable Consumption and the Law." *Environmental Law* 27 (4): 1243–93.

Sappington, David E., and Dennis L. Weisman. 1996. *Designing Incentive Regulation for the Telecommunications Industry*. Cambridge and Washington, D.C.: MIT Press and AEI Press.

Scherer, F. Michael. 1994. *Competition Policies for an Integrated World Economy*. Washington, D.C.: Brookings Institution.

Slovic, Paul, Baruch Fischoff, and Sarah Lichtenstein. 1985. "Regulation of Risk: A Psychological Perspective." In Roger G. Noll, ed., *Regulatory Policy and the Social Sciences*. Berkeley: University of California Press.

Smith, V. Kerry, ed. 1984. *Environmental Policy under Reagan's Executive Order: The Role of Benefit-Cost Analysis*. Chapel Hill: University of North Carolina Press.

Smith, Vernon L. 1987. "Currents of Competition in Electricity Markets." *Regulation* 11 (March/April): 23–29.

———. 1996. "Electric Power Deregulation." *Regulation* 19 (1): 33–46.

Sunstein, Cass R. 1996. "Congress, Constitutional Moments, and the Cost-Benefit State." *Stanford Law Review* 48 (2): 247–310.

Tengs, Tammy O., and John D. Graham. 1996. "The Opportunity Costs of Haphazard Social Investments in Life-Saving." In Robert W. Hahn, ed., *Risks, Costs, and Lives Saved: Getting Better Results from Regulation*. New York and Washington, D.C.: Oxford University Press and AEI Press.

Tengs, Tammy, Miriam E. Adams, Joseph S. Pliskin, Dana Gelb Safran, Joanna E.

Siegel, Michael C. Weinstein, and John D. Graham. 1994. *Five Hundred Life-Saving Interventions and Their Cost-Effectiveness.* Cambridge: Harvard Center for Risk Analysis.

Tierney, John. 1996. "Recycling Is Garbage." *New York Times Magazine,* June 30.

United Kingdom, Deregulation Unit. 1997. *Cutting Red Tape: The Government's Deregulation Campaign.* London: Cabinet Office, Deregulation Unit.

U.S. National Center for Health Statistics, Center for Disease Control and Prevention. 1995. *Monthly Vital Statistics Report: Advance Report of Final Mortality Statistics, 1992* 43 (6), supplement.

U.S. Shadow Financial Regulatory Committee. 2000. *Reforming Bank Capital Regulation: A Proposal by the U.S. Shadow Financial Regulatory Committee.* Washington, D.C.: AEI Press.

Van Bergeijk, P. A. G., and R. C. G. Haffner. 1995. *Deregulation, Privatisation, and the Macroeconomy: Measurement, Modeling, and Policy.* Cheltenham, England: Edward Elgar.

Van Houtven, George L., and Maureen L. Cropper. 1994. "When Is a Life Too Costly to Save?" Policy Research Working Paper 1260. Washington. D.C.: World Bank, Environment, Infrastructure, and Agriculture Department.

Van Sinderen, J., P. A. G. Van Bergeijk, R. C. G. Haffner, and P. M. Waasdorp. 1994. "De Kosten van Economische Verstarring op Macro-Niveau." *Economisch Statistiche Berichten* 79: 3954.

Virginia Department of Planning and Budget. 1997. "Comprehensive Review of Existing State Regulations." Richmond: Virginia Department of Planning and Budget.

Viscusi, W. Kip. 1992. *Fatal Tradeoffs: Public and Private Responsibilities for Risks.* New York: Oxford University Press.

———. 1993. "The Value of Risks to Life and Health." *Journal of Economic Literature* 31 (December): 1912–46.

———. 1996. "The Dangers of Unbounded Commitments to Regulate Risk." In Robert W. Hahn, ed., *Risks, Costs, and Lives Saved: Getting Better Results from Regulation.* New York and Washington, D.C.: Oxford University Press and AEI Press.

Viscusi, W. Kip, and Wesley A. Magat. 1987. *Learning about Risk.* Cambridge: Harvard University Press.

Vogelsang, Ingo, and Bridger M. Mitchell. 1997. *Telecommunications Competition: The Last Ten Miles.* Cambridge and Washington, D.C.: MIT Press and AEI Press.

Weidenbaum, Murray. 1997. "Regulatory Process Reform." *Regulation* (Winter): 20–26.

Weidenbaum, Murray, and Robert DeFina. 1978. *The Cost of Federal Regulation of Economic Activity.* American Enterprise Institute Reprint No. 88. Washington, D.C.: American Enterprise Institute.

White, Lawrence J. 1981. *Reforming Regulation: Processes and Problems.* Englewood Cliffs, N.J.: Prentice-Hall.

———. 1996. "Competition versus Harmonization—An Overview of International Regulation of Financial Services." In Claude E. Barfield, ed., *International Financial Markets.* Washington, D.C.: AEI Press.

———. 1999. *U.S. Public Policy toward Network Industries.* Washington, D.C.: AEI-

Brookings Joint Center for Regulatory Studies, American Enterprise Institute and Brookings Institution.

Wilson, Pete. 1996. California Executive Order W-131-96. Sacramento, Calif.: Office of the Governor.

Winston, Clifford. 1993. "Economic Deregulation: Days of Reckoning for Microeconomists." *Journal of Economic Literature* 31 (September): 1263–89.

———. 1998. "U.S. Industry Adjustment to Economic Deregulation." *Journal of Economic Perspectives* 12 (Summer): 89–110.

Winston, Clifford, and Steven Morrison. 1998. "Fundamental Flaws of Social Regulation: The Case of Airplane Noise." AEI-Brookings Joint Center Working Paper 98-02.

World Bank. 1992. *World Development Report 1992: Development and Environment.* Washington, D.C.: World Bank.

———. 1994. "Chile—Managing Environmental Problems: Economic Analysis of Selected Issues." Report No. 13061-CH, Environment and Urban Development Division, Country Department I, Latin America and the Caribbean Region. Washington, D.C.: World Bank.

———. 1995. *Bureaucrats in Business: The Economics and Politics of Government Ownership.* Washington, D.C.: World Bank.

———. 1996. *World Development Report 1996: From Plan to Market.* Washington, D.C.: World Bank.

"The World Economy Survey." 1996. *Economist* 340 (September 28): 1–46.

World Trade Organization. 1996. *United States—Standards for Reformulated and Conventional Gasoline: Appellate Body Report and Panel Report.* Decision by the WTO Dispute Settlement Body, Appellate Body Report AB-1996-1.

Wriston, Walter B. 1992. *The Twilight of Sovereignty: How the Information Revolution Is Transforming Our World.* New York: Scribner.

Index

Accountability, regulatory, 26 t, 69–70
Accountable Pipeline Safety and
    Partnership Act of 1996, 28 t
Agriculture, Department of, 35, 36 t,
    42 t, 48 f, 58 t, 62 t
Airline sector deregulation, 82 n. 38
Anderson, Robert, and colleagues, 10
Argentina, 11, 70
Arizona, 30 t
Australia, 3, 11, 12 t, 13–16 f,
    23–24 t, 31, 69, 81 n. 28, 82 n. 38
Austria, 13–16 f, 23 t

Backsliding, 71–72
Balancing statutes, 28 t
  definition, 44
  requirements, 54–55, 56 t
Bank of International Settlements, 76
Base year of implementation, 39,
    45–46, 52
Basil Accord, 76
Belgium, 14–16 f
Benefit-cost analysis, 69
Benefit-cost ratio
  defined, 46

regression, 53–54
Benefit-cost test, 3, 4, 5, 44, 55,
    57–59
  methodology for analysis, 38–41
Benefits and costs, 5, 9–13, 20–21, 35
  balancing, legislation, 28 t
  information cataloged by regulatory
    agencies, 61, 62 t
  methodology for estimating, 38–41
  See also Net benefits
Bliley, Thomas J., Jr., survey of agency
    costs, 60–62
Britain, 3
Bush administration, 72

Cable News Network effect, 67
California, 30 t, 32
Canada, 12 t, 13–16 f, 23–24 t, 74,
    80 n. 22, 82 n. 38
Cancer risks and regulations, 40,
    47–48, 50, 51 f
Carter, Jimmy, 89 n. 43
Chile, 1, 17–20 f, 70, 81 n. 29
China, 1, 81 n. 29
Clean Air Act, 25, 37 t, 41, 43 t, 44,

52, 54, 55, 58–59, 87 n. 20
Clean Air Act Amendments
  of 1977, 9
  of 1990, 32
Clean Water Act, 37 t, 43 t, 44, 52,
  58 t
Climate change, 67
Clinton administration, 72
Clinton's Executive Order 12866, 26 t,
  34, 60, 84 n. 4, 85 n. 11, 87 n. 21
Code of Federal Regulations, 61
Commerce, Department of, 62 t
Commodity Futures Trading
  Commission, 62 t
Communication, impact of
  globalization on, 66, 67
Competition, 17
  policy, 70–71
Compliance costs, 86 n. 16
Comprehensive Environmental
  Response, Cooperation, and
  Liability Act, 37 t, 41, 43 t, 44, 58 t
Congress, 25, 52, 54, 64
Consumer Product Safety
  Commission, 35, 36 t, 42 t, 48 f,
  58 t, 61, 62 t, 87 n. 21
Cost-effectiveness, 69, 90 n. 44,
  90 n. 45, 93 n. 69
  defined, 46
  of environmental, health
  and safety regulations, 46, 48 f,
  49 t, 51 f
  regression, 46–54
Costs
  outside the United States, 11, 13
  problems with estimates of, 10–11
  See also Benefits and costs
Costs savings, 86 n. 16
Council of Economic Advisers, 64

Delaney Clause, 25, 28 t
Denmark, 14–16 f, 18
Discount rate, 39–40, 44, 46 t, 47 f
Distribution, problems of
  deregulation, 71

East European countries, 1, 70
Economic analysis
  impact on regulatory agencies, 60
  role in future, 71
  role in regulatory reform, 69,
  85 n. 12
Economic information, compilation
  of, 69
Economic regulation and deregulation,
  31
  benefits of, 10, 12 t
  defined, 7
  future of, 70–71, 77–78
  rationale for, 7–8
  trends in, 13–19
Egypt, 17–20 f
Energy, Department of, 62 t
Entry restrictions in OECD countries,
  15 f
Environmental Protection Agency,
  35, 36–37 t, 48 f, 49 t, 50, 52, 55,
  57, 58 t, 59, 60, 61, 62 t, 85 n. 12,
  88 n. 32
  and cancer risk, 47, 51
  net benefits of regulations, 41–44
  quantitative analyses, 34
  regulations less efficient, 50, 53
Environmental statutes regulatory
  scorecard, 37t
Europe (selected countries), 11,
  17–18, 74
European Community, 18, 20, 74, 75
European Union, 12 t
Evans, Lewis, and colleagues, 11
Executive orders, *see* Clinton, Reagan

Factor mobility, 66, 67
Family and Medical Leave Act of
  1993, 83 n. 47
Federal Communications
  Commission, 62 t
Federal Deposit Insurance
  Corporation, 62 t
Federal Energy Regulatory
  Commission, 62 t

Federal Highway Administration, 61
Federal Insecticide, Fungicide, and
    Rodenticide Act, 37 t, 43 t, 44,
    58 t, 95 n. 86
Federal Register, 32, 39, 40
Federal Reserve Board, 62 t
Federal Trade Commission, 62 t
Finland, 14–16 f, 23 t
Food and Drug Administration, 62 t,
    73
Food Quality Protection Act of 1996,
    25, 28 t
France, 13 f, 74, 81 nn. 24, 30
Free trade and harmonization, 74–76
Future
    of economic deregulation, 77–78
    of regulation, 70–73
    of regulatory reform, 5

Germany, 12 t, 13–16 f, 23 t, 74,
    81 n. 24
Ghana, 17–20 f
Global organizations, future, 76
Globalization
    definition, 66
    future, 76
    impact on regulation, 66–68
Government intervention, 68–69
Government Performance and Results
    Act of 1993, 83 n. 59, 97 n. 104
GNP test, 47–48
Greece, 19
Grubb, David, and William Wells, 18

Hahn, Robert W., 10, 61
    Hahn regression, 48–51
    Hahn-Morrall regression, 49–52
    Hahn-Morrall/OIRA regression,
        49–50
Hahn, Robert W., and John Hird, 3, 9
Harmonization and free trade, 74–76
Health Care Financing Administration,
    87 n. 27
Health and Human Services,
    Department of, 35, 36 t, 41, 42 t,

48 f, 58 t, 93 n. 68
Health Insurance Portability and
    Accountability Act of 1996,
    83 n. 47
Hopkins, Thomas D., 9, 20
Housing and Urban Development,
    Department of, 35, 36 t, 42 t, 48 f,
    58 t, 62 t
Howard, Philip, 3, 32

Iceland, 23 t
India, 17–20 f
International Union, UAW v. OSHA,
    95 n. 82
Internet, 2, 64
Ireland, 14–16 f, 18
Italy, 13 f

Japan, 11, 12 t, 13–16 f, 23 t, 70, 74,
    80 n. 22, 81 nn. 24, 28

Korea, 17–20 f

Labor, Department of, health and
    safety rules, 36 t, 41, 42 t, 48 f,
    50, 58 t
Labor markets
    future of regulation of, 74
    and globalization, 66
    regulation of, 18–21

Markets, international, 66
Massachusetts, 30 t
McGovern, George, 3
Mexico, 1, 3, 17–20 f, 23–24 t, 29,
    69, 74, 75
Monetization of benefits, 35, 36–37 t,
    39, 57
Morrall, John F., 48, 53
    Hahn-Morrall regression, 49–52

National Association on
    Administrative Rules Review, 25
National Highway Traffic Safety
    Administration, 39, 60, 61, 62 t,

93 n. 68

National Performance Review, 27 t, 72

Net benefits
for environmental statutes, 43 t
of final rules over time, 44, 45 f
as a function of discount rate, 46–47
of regulation, totals, 38, 41–47

Netherlands, 12 t, 13 f, 23 t, 81 n. 30

New York, 30 t

New Zealand, 11, 14–16 f, 19, 23 t, 81 n. 28, 82 n. 38

North American Free Trade Agreement, 74, 75

Norway, 14–16 f, 23 t

Nuclear Regulatory Commission, 61, 62 t, 87 n. 21

Occupational Safety and Health Act, 54, 55

Occupational Safety and Health Administration, 4, 35, 59, 60, 61, 62 t

OECD countries, 13–16, 22, 29, 30

Office of Information and Regulatory Affairs, 47, 50, 52, 89 n. 43, 92 n. 54

Office of Management and Budget, 26 t, 27 t, 33, 64, 69–70

OIRA regression, 49–50

Organization for Economic Cooperation and Development, 11
See also OECD countries

Oversight, regulatory, 22, 23–24 t, 30 t, 31

Paperwork Reduction Act of 1980, 89 n. 43

Philippines, 17–20 f

Pipeline Safety and Partnership Act, 25

Policy recommendations, 63–64

Political affiliation, effect on cost-effectiveness estimates, 93 n. 69

Pollution, 59, 68, 94 n. 71

abatement expenditures, 11, 13 f
air, reduction benefits, 40 t

Portugal, 23 t

Price restrictions, in OECD countries, 17 f

Privatization, 13–15, 31
in OECD countries, 14 f

Process regulation, 35
defined, 7
future of, 73, 78
reforms of, 22–25

Product industries, in developing countries
ownership of, 19 f
regulation of, 20 f

Reagan's Executive Order 12291, 34, 60, 84 n. 4, 85 n. 12, 87 n. 21

Regulation
alternative, 21–22, 72–73
economic and political problems with, 8–9, 10, 11
efficiency of, relative, 46–54
impact on economy, 63
prioritizing, 52
rationale for, 7–8
reforms of, worldwide, 14
review of activity, 26–27 t
steps to improve reform of, 63–64
understanding effects of, 68–69
See also Economic regulation, Process regulation, Social regulation

Regulatory agencies, see specific title

Regulatory impact analysis, 32, 38–41, 84 n. 4, 85 n. 11
impact on regulatory process, 57, 60–61, 96 n. 89
quality of, 34–35
time-frame specification, 40–41

Regulatory scorecard, 1981 to mid-1996, 36 t, 37 t

Resources Conservation and Recovery Act, 37 t, 43 t, 55, 58 t

Revolution, regulatory, 1–2, 3–4

RIA, see Regulatory impact analysis

Safe Drinking Water Act, 37 t, 43 t, 44, 58 t
Safe Drinking Water Act Amendments of 1966, 28 t
Securities and Exchange Commission, 62 t
Senegal, 17–20 f
Service industries, in developing countries
  ownership of, 17 f
  regulation of, 18 f
Small Business Regulatory Enforcement Fairness Act of 1996, 26 t
Social regulation, 3–5, 31
  benefits of, 10
  benefits and costs of, in United States, 21–22
  costs, outside United States, 11
  defined, 7
  future of, 71–73, 78
  growth of, 21–22
  impact of globalization on, 67, 68
Soviet Union, 1
Spain, 14–16 f, 19
Standards, international
  harmonization of, 75–76
State regulatory reforms, 25, 29, 30 t
Statutory restrictions on regulations, 35, 54–55
Supermandate provision, 54
Surface Transportation Board, 62 t
Sweden, 14–16 f, 23–24 t
Switzerland, 14–16 f

Telecommunications Act of 1996, 27 t

Time trend for benefits and rules, 44, 45 f
Toxic Substances Control Act, 37 t, 43 t, 44, 58 t, 95 n. 86
Transportation, Department of, 36 t, 39, 41, 42 t, 44, 48 f, 58 t, 61
Turkey, 14–16 f, 17–20 f

Uganda, 1
Unfunded Mandates Reform Act of 1995, 25, 26 t, 96 n. 88
United Kingdom, 13–16 f, 23–24 t, 69, 71, 81 n. 24, 82 n. 38
United States, 4, 9, 12 t, 13–16 f, 31, 69, 71, 73, 74, 75, 78, 81 n. 30
  costs of social regulation in, 20–21
  first to initiate reforms, 2–3, 15, 25
  future of social regulation in, 71–72, 77
  labor markets, 16–18, 74
  overview of reform, 23–24 t
  privatization in, 14, 15 f
  review of regulatory activity in, 26–27 t
U.S. Department of, *see specific title*

Value of benefits, 44, 46 t, 59–60
Value of life, 39–40, 59–60
Virginia, 30 t
Viscusi, W. Kip, 39

Wealth, increase in, worldwide, 68
Welfare gains, 11
Willingness-to-pay values, 39
Winston, Clifford, 3, 10
World Trade Organization, 2, 74–75

About the Author

Robert W. Hahn is the director of the AEI-Brookings Joint Center for Regulatory Studies, a resident scholar at the American Enterprise Institute, and a research associate at Harvard University. He previously served as a senior staff member of the Council of Economic Advisers for two years. The editor of *Risks, Costs, and Lives Saved: Getting Better Results from Regulation*, Mr. Hahn frequently contributes to general-interest periodicals and leading scholarly journals, including the *New York Times*, the *Wall Street Journal*, the *American Economic Review*, and the *Yale Law Journal*. He has been a consultant to government and industry on a variety of issues involving regulation and privatization. In addition, Mr. Hahn is the cofounder of the Community Preparatory School, an inner-city middle school in Providence, Rhode Island, that provides opportunities for disadvantaged youth to achieve their full potential.

JOINT CENTER

AEI-BROOKINGS JOINT CENTER FOR REGULATORY STUDIES

www.ingramcontent.com/pod-product-compliance
Lightning Source LLC
Jackson TN
JSHW011940131224
75386JS00041B/1474